I Remember St Petersburg

I Remember St Petersburg

E. M. Almedingen

Illustrations by John Sergeant

The Kazan Cathedral

LONGMANS YOUNG BOOKS

Longmans Young Books Ltd
London and Harlow
Associated Companies, Branches and Representatives
throughout the world

SBN: 582 15505 3

Printed in Great Britain
by Ebenezer Baylis and Son Ltd
The Trinity Press, Worcester, and London

Contents

St Nicholas' Cathedral

Author's Note

I make no apology for choosing a title which—on the surface,
is about as fresh as last year's snow. Names of cities do get
changed, and there is no reason why they should not—provided
that there exist good grounds for the change. St Petersburg, that
surprising and lovely city, had its christening on a May morning
in 1703. That beginning was a tremendous act of faith on the
part of its creator because who could have imagined a great
nation's capital arising out of a swamp? Yet the city, once
founded, was named, and the old name lives on in more than
dusty records and yellowed maps. It is a German name, and that
expressed the chief purpose of Peter the Great—to bring his
people into the Western fellowship. Whether he succeeded or
not lies outside the scope of this book. Its aim is to bring you as
close as possible to Peter's own city. Also to revive a child's
memories of a life that used to be lived there, a life sharply in-
formed by wind and water, full of gaiety and surprise, though
often enough chequered by danger and a sense of terror in the
distance, but never a dull life, all its days spiced by the unexpected. The very poverty in St Petersburg wore a cloak of
many vivid colours.

E. M. Almedingen

June, 1968

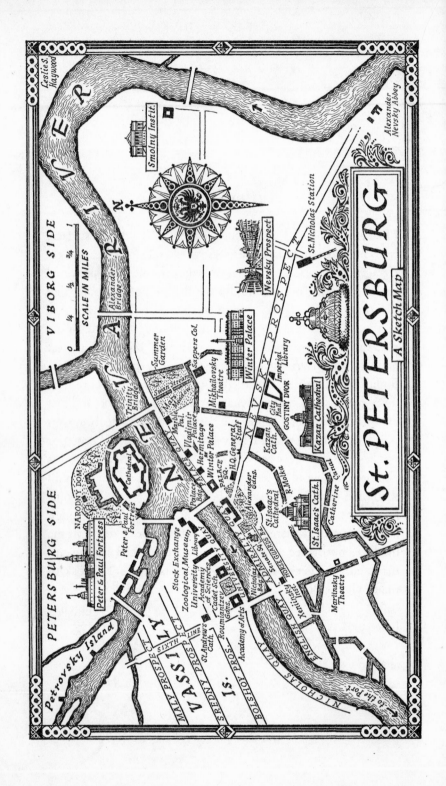

Mariinsky Theatre

CHAPTER ONE

The Beginnings

I WAS born in St Petersburg, in a big flat not far from the Mariinsky Theatre, in the summer of 1898. My arrival should have been in September at my Danish grandmother's house in the very depths of Finland, but a terrific storm, raging all over the city for a night and a day, sent me into the world two months earlier. As I grew up, I felt deeply grateful to that storm: I would not have been born anywhere except in St Petersburg.

Now, on my fifth birthday, I had—among other presents—an enamelled mug given me. At first its contents (chocolate drops) interested me far more than the mug iteslf. But the sweets were eaten soon enough and the mug remained. On one side it had the familiar picture of Peter the Great in workman's clothes, a big hammer in his hand. On the other side, surrounding a tiny picture of the city, ran the words 'Bicentenary of St Petersburg—1703–1903'. Little by little, that mug became my first history text-book. By the time I was seven, St Petersburg's exciting beginnings were as clear to me as the dark blue waters of the river Neva in mid-summer. It was a story that gripped me from first to last, and I began to realize that its richly coloured past belonged to me—and I to it—as much as the present did. I found no difficulty in seeing the lovely city rise out of the swampy nineteen islands huddled together near the estuary where the queenly river ran into the Gulf of Finland.

Peter the Great, the founder, became my hero and his new capital—the greatest wonder of the world. Before I reached my tenth birthday, the beginnings of St Petersburg had become a gorgeously illuminated scroll. Some of the knowledge came from books but most of it, I think, reached me and won my affection by means of unending 'wanders' from one island to another. Not a building did I see but it offered enough to stir the imagination and in this way I learnt the story of St Petersburg and its beginnings which I would like now to share with my readers.

*

It happened in May 1703. The Great Northern War between Sweden and Russia had already started, and the Russians had been badly beaten at Narva, but not all the dice were loaded in favour of Sweden. Peter had his eye on a wide river born of Lake Ladoga in the east and falling into the Gulf of Finland in the west. Close to the wide estuary lay a huddle of some nine-

teen islands, a few inhabited by Finnish fishermen, the rest—
so many mossy swamps, granite boulders and starved firs
scattered here and there. Sweden, however, had a lien on the
river Neva, and she had built two grim forts, one near the
estuary, the other to the east.

It was hardly a promising spot for Peter's 'window to the
West', but he chose it.

Lightning-swift, he dislodged the Swedes from the forts, and
within a few months thousands and thousands of labourers
were rushed to the north from Central Russia. All the available
transport by land and water was mobilized to bring building
material to the little islands. Dutch, Scottish, English and
German engineers were engaged to drain the swamps, and the
Herculean task was made all the harder by the demands of war,
the ineptitude of native workmen, and the whims of the
climate—fogs, floods, storms, bitter cold and terrific heat.

But the work was done. On a May day in 1703 Peter laid
the foundation stone of the first church, St Samson's, on Viborg
Side, an island on the North Bank of the Neva. His own 'palace',
a timbered cottage of six rooms, was already finished; there his
wife, Catherine, darned his hose and pickled cucumbers and
lemons for his dinner. In 1906, when I was about eight, I
entered it for the first time and held my breath for sheer amazement. It was a working man's home; the rooms were poky,
the ceilings low, the furniture of the roughest kind. It was an
experience to touch the back of an oaken chair, and so much
of my 'feel' for the past of the city came in some such way.

In 1703 a tangled wilderness stretched behind the 'palace'.
Soon the wilderness was turned into the first pleasance of the
new capital, the Summer Gardens with their famous avenue
of limes, the first park I knew where I walked first with a
nurse, then with a maid, often running away from her with
my hoop, and, finally, by myself. Every tree carried a breath

Peter the Grea

of history, and a favourite game was to guess which among the old, wide-boughed limes had been planted by Peter the Great himself.

He had had a tiny cottage for his use. Not so his ministers. A stroll down the First Line of Vassily Island brought me face to face with an enormous mansion, once the palace of Prince Menshikov, Peter's Prime Minister, and a military school in my time, and not far from it, fronting the Neva, were the exquisite buildings of the University where Peter had had his government offices. The long, vaulted cloister was never shut. When I was little, the maid in charge of me complained that the cloister gave her 'the creeps'. 'Far too many shadows about,' she grumbled, but to me those very shadows stood for so many links between my small self and the city's beginnings.

The first Cathedral of St Peter and St Paul reared its spires and cupolas on an adjoining island. More and more stone houses were built during Peter's reign and more and more people of substance would leave Moscow to settle in St Petersburg. 'And how did they travel?' I once asked my eldest brother. 'There were no trains then—or were there?'

'Trains?' he laughed. 'There was not even a road—just forests and swamps. The road to Moscow is not as old as St Petersburg.'

My knowledge of geography being rather thin in 1905, I imagined that road to be like the great Nevsky Prospect, the longest avenue in the world, its length stretching for five miles, its width equalling that of three ordinary streets. The avenue ended at the gates of the first Abbey in St Petersburg, dedicated to St Alexander Nevsky, a prince of Novgorod, who in the thirteenth century had defeated the Swedes on the ice-shackled Neva. His shrine was brought to St Petersburg, he being named patron of the new capital.

Its sanctuaries grew in number from year to year, but St Petersburg never lost a pagan imprint. The superb waterfront spoke of a remote Scandinavian past and, having once seen a picture of it, I could easily imagine a Viking ship cutting through the deep-blue waters of the Neva. The wide streets seemed strange to any true-bred Russian. The very colours belonged to a Scandinavian landscape: pale violet, faint green, pearl-grey. Its climate certainly called for hardihood, but its winds and waters made short shrift of so many unpleasing smells to be found in other Russian cities.

The Neva reigns supreme, but she has four large tributaries and numberless little rivers. At first, the young city had no bridges and people crossed from one island to another in hired boats unless they were wealthy enough to have barges of their own. Yet even all that mass of running water did not satisfy Peter the Great: he had a number of canals dug all over the islands, and in my childhood there were a hundred and fifty bridges.

*

Day by day, month by month, I went on learning the story, and I was fortunate in my teacher: he was my father's elder brother, a soldier by profession, a publisher of children's books and periodicals by inheritance, and a lover of St Petersburg by personal choice. A busy man, he could not often spare the time to take a small and inquisitive niece for a walk, but his collection of old engravings, maps and plans of the city was like a house of many windows to me. There was a very frail plan of Vassily Island, its wide streets known as Lines studded all over with incredibly trim firs. There was an engraving of the Empress Elizabeth, Peter the Great's daughter, wearing a soldier's cloak and holding an absurdly small sword. There was an engraving of the Neva, spanned by two bridges and crowded by tiny rowing boats. There were so many others, each telling

Empress Elizabeth

B

a story and deepening my affection for the city, as little by little, its past wove itself into my present.

There was one golden occasion when my uncle Alexis had a whole day of leisure and wrote to say that I was to meet him by the Academy of Sciences on Vassily Island. I think it was in the summer of 1907, and didn't I pray for the fine weather to continue? We met by the grand entrance, and he asked at once:

'Who founded the Academy?'

I thought hard. I knew it was an Empress—but I was not at all sure which.

'Catherine,' I brought out at last.

'Which? There were two of them.'

'Peter's wife,' I ventured, and he laughed.

'Both had Peters for their husbands. It was Catherine I, but she died in 1727, and St Petersburg might well have perished.'

'Perished?'

'Yes,' said my uncle, 'I will tell you about it at lunch.'

We fed on the Neva, on board a small restaurant barge moored to one of several jetties. Tables were set on deck.

But after we were seated I had to wait until my uncle had finished ordering the meal before he would go on. Even a modest lunch on board one of the barges was a rare treat, but my mind could not concentrate on food.

'Might have perished?' I echoed and watched him crumble a roll.

'How old are you?' he flashed at me.

'I'll be nine in July.'

'Then you should know your history.'

'But I do! I do!' I cried.

'Not enough. The great Peter's grandson, Peter II, came to the throne in 1727, and he hated St Petersburg. He preferred Moscow. He was in his early teens when he became Emperor. . . .'

18

Food forgotten, I listened. I heard about the boy taking his court and government to Moscow, and leaving his grandfather's city to fend for itself. All work came to a standstill in the shipyards and steel works, moss and grass grew in every street, timbered houses tumbled down and there were no labourers to rebuild them. The pulse of trade fell to such a low ebb that people, unable to get much provender at the markets, took to fishing in the river. St Petersburg was an orphaned city.

'For how long?' I breathed.

'Nearly three years,' answered my uncle. 'Then fortunately the boy died, and the city rose up again. His successor, Anna, was so keen on establishing it that she all but ruined the treasury. And that,' said my uncle, folding his napkin, 'is enough history for today.'

So that golden hallmark came and went—but something remained, and on my ninth birthday my uncle sent me a gorgeously bound and illustrated history of St Petersburg. The binding was superb. The illustrations—so many highly coloured daubs, but that did not prevent me from recognizing familiar landmarks. The text was most illuminating. I learnt that Peter the Great's daughter, Elizabeth, who reigned from 1741-1761, was certainly a landmark in herself. She built much and wisely, often employing foreign talent and labour. The few factories established by her father grew tenfold. Two printing works were founded by her, and I delighted in the picture of the first bookshop attached to the Academy of Sciences, the wall a rather incredible pink and the low door a wild green. A whole page was devoted to the almshouses (no longer extant in my day), their flat roofs coloured bright crimson, but the text did not mention their whereabouts.

There were quite a few Elizabethan mansions still standing when I was a child. They looked most imposing with their colonnaded porches and finely proportioned windows. Yet I read that their inhabitants enjoyed little comfort; the ground floors had great state apartments where dances and banquets were given. The rest of the mansions consisted of little rooms serving as bedrooms on the first floor, and garrets above, for the servants. 'All the chimneys smoked,' I read, 'and the continual damp led to fungi sprouting up and down the walls.' It seemed that foreign skill was much too expensive. At the foot of the page was a picture of a rather drunkenly leaning house, its windows put in anyhow and not a single chimney stack seen on the roof. As if to stress the ugliness, the picture was all in muted drab colours, with a dash of sad grey here and there. The caption said: 'This house was erected by a Russian builder who had forgotten to put in either a staircase or a chimney.'

I liked best the chapter about St Petersburg under Catherine the Great (1762–1796). Here, in spite of the grotesque colours, were no legends but satisfying facts, and the picture of the Hermitage interior was indeed true in all details—the great staircase, the malachite pillars, the spacious halls housing collections of pictures, statuary, trifles of ivory, jade from all corners of the world. On the last page I came on a picture of the Empress in a plain grey gown and a white cap, examining a set of chessmen. That was pleasing indeed, since I had seen that set and admired it on my first visit to the Hermitage when I was eight. The Hermitage, joined to the Winter Palace by a winged gallery, was far more than a museum, the first of its kind in Russia. Catherine the Great instructed her agents all over Europe to find treasures and to buy them at the lowest possible prices. She considered her vast collection not in terms of personal property but as a national inheritance.

The book ended with four illustrations, no captions to any of them, but each page bore a date drawn in bold scarlet and gold: 19th February 1861. The first showed the belfry of the Kazan Cathedral, the bellringers exerting themselves to the utmost, with great jugs of beer standing against a wall. The second had an open sledge, drawn by a single horse, with two officers in fur-edged cloaks acknowledging the bows of an immense crowd. However crude the drawing, I recognized the Emperor Alexander II and his eldest son. The third page was devoted to a scene near a market place with men and women, incongruously dressed in bright summer clothes, dancing on the hard-beaten snow. Finally, the unknown artist let himself go entirely when painting the illuminations all along the great waterfront: scarlet wheels shot up to be cut by vividly green swords. Every colour and shade of the rainbow were thrown together in an amazing confusion.

The date explained it all: the joy of the city on the day when serfdom became a thing of the past, when strangers, as I read elsewhere, would embrace one another in the streets, people danced in the open, and the immense waterfront was illuminated all through that long wintry night in February 1861.

I did not go to school until 1913 when I was 15, but I had tutors for an hour or two in the mornings, all of them penurious and shabby university students, far poorer than we were. They snatched at any opportunity to earn a few roubles a month by teaching a most unpromising pupil whose attention never came to life except during history lessons. Yet, if I learned badly, they certainly did not shine as teachers. I disliked them all because they were sarcastic about the city of my birth, with its matchless skies and waters, because a plate of cabbage soup and a rissole eaten in the university canteen meant far more than an apple or a slice of dry bread enjoyed whilst watching the sunlight ripple over the Neva. Their penury I respected. Their wooden outlook repelled me. To them, any building, however exquisite, was just a building, not a paean in stone.

When one of them, who taught me rags and wisps of history (he read biology in college), said that the greatest mistake of

Peter I was to found St Petersburg, I reined in my anger as best I could and later felt shamelessly relieved when I heard of his arrest owing to activities which had nothing to do with biology and included the distribution of bombs.

The lessons over, the rest of the day belonged to me. From 1906 on, that is when I was eight, I took to endless 'wanders' from one island to another. Seldom enough did I have money for a boat or a horse tram, but walking was good whatever the weather. Each day enlarged my knowledge of and deepened my affection for the city.

My well-nigh daily 'wanders' often led to the Summer Gardens, planted by Peter the Great and one of the loveliest pleasances in the city. Halfway down the wide lime avenue I would come to a fairly large space fringed all round by firs and elms. It went by the name of 'children's corner'. In the middle was a bronze statue of an old man seated in a comfortable chair. The monument was surrounded by high wrought-iron railings, with mice, cats, dogs, monkeys, bears, wolves and squirrels treading a measure all round the monument raised in honour of Ivan Krylov, Russia's famous fabulist, a peer of Aesop and La Fontaine. Krylov had three loves in his long life: St Petersburg, children and animals. He used to say 'such a city would have inspired Homer'. Whenever I came near, and that was often enough, I could not but think of a very thin and tattered sheet of paper covered with almost illegible writing which had a place of honour among our treasures: a fable of Krylov's scribbled at the table of a great aunt of mine, Elizabeth Olenina, née Poltoralzky. The family story went that Krylov had written it whilst waiting to be served with a chicken pie. As soon as the plate was before him, the paper fell on the floor and was later retrieved by his hostess.

'Keep it, dear friend,' the old man told her. 'Ah—but it was a good pie!'

As I grew older, my wanderings took me further and further afield, past the Senate Square, through Alexander Gardens, to the very edge of Nevsky Prospect. About a mile further, with an exquisite flower garden gracing its front, stood the Kazan Cathedral, the most important sanctuary of St Petersburg. There, in the nave, with bullet-riddled regimental colours hanging over it, stood a simple grey stone grave dear to every Russian heart. The great Kutuzov lay there, who, aged over 70, saved Russia from Napoleon's clutches in 1812. He was a countryman born and bred, but no higher honour could be paid him than to lay him down in the very heart of the capital, and even a brief visit conjured up pictures that few history books could have given me.

On really red-letter days I would take the tram to carry me right through Nevsky Prospect to Nicholas station. Past its hustle and bustle, I would find myself walking along a different Nevsky, some of its crazily-timbered houses going back to the eighteenth century. Farther on, to my right I saw the great gateway of the Alexander Nevsky Abbey. In one of its many cloisters, close to St Lazarus' Church, I came on a slab laid flush with the flagstones. Three words were chiselled on it: 'Here lies Suvorov'. The greatest Russian field-marshal, who had Kutozov and many others among his pupils, loathed ostentation and the simple inscription was in accordance with his own wishes. He had been loaded with titles and honours of all kinds. He wanted none of them remembered after his death.

Yet the foremost among all the sons of St Petersburg was Pushkin, Russia's greatest poet. He was born in the country and buried there, too, though he died in the city in 1837. But St Petersburg, where he lived for many years, was the greatest love of his life, and he was the first to sing of her beauty in truly incomparable lines about the Neva and all the lesser waters, about her palaces and hovels, the grace of the white

Admiralty buildings and the majesty of the Bronze Rider, and about her white nights when:

I can read and write without a candle,
With a dawn breaking through a sunset.

Her high winds, her anger, her legends, all alike inspired him, and my veneration for him was deepened by intimate links. First, one of Pushkin's loveliest lyrics was written to a member of my family. Next, and even more important, he was a friend of my grandfather, Serge Poltoralzky, himself a man of letters. A copy of Walter Scott's *Antiquary*, once belonging to Pushkin, lay on the shelf, together with the proofs of his poem *The Bronze Rider* and the drama *Boris Godunov*, both given by him to my grandfather because 'I value your judgment so much'. Pushkin died in St Petersburg in 1837, but to me he lived within all the beauty so prodigally lavished by the city.

The brilliant galaxy of St Petersburg's stars did not end with Pushkin. Nearly all the great novelists of the nineteenth century found their steading there. Gogol, an unmoneyed civil service clerk, started his work in a badly heated, ill-lit garret in one of the city's humbler streets. Dostoyevsky, though aware of her splendours, was not afraid to turn the torch of his genius towards her darkest corners. She had many of them. St Petersburg's secret music was echoed in the works of Glynka, Mussorgsky, Tchaikovsky and other composers. Russia never produced painters of a world-wide reputation, but such as there were— for instance, Serov, Repin and Aivasovsky—lived in St Petersburg, but though they must have been aware of her magic, they could not interpret it. The colour of her distances alone would have demanded the genius of a Giorgione or a Leonardo.

One other modest name should be added here—that of Staniukovich, sailor, novelist, and true lover of St Petersburg. He is little known, yet at least one of his novels, *The Islanders*,

Nikolai Gogol

paid fitting tribute to the city that bred him. It is all about Vassily Island and its people, mostly humble folk, minor civil servants and the like who lived in cheap flats, took great care of their clothes, regarded a bottle of wine on their table as a major event in their lives, endured the climatic vagaries without a murmur, and were pleased when able to afford a pair of kid gloves for their hard-working, uncomplaining wives. A grey background, but thinly streaked with colour, and yet it succeeded in answering the island's landscape.

CHAPTER TWO

People of Mark Met and Heard About

MY PEOPLE were a clan rather than a family, but not all of them lived in St Petersburg and certainly very few of them, my uncle Alexis excepted, took much notice of 'the poor relations', to whom I belonged. My father left us before I was two years old, and the grand flat with its ballroom and two drawing-rooms was exchanged in 1900 for a very modest home on Vassily Island, a home kept by my mother, who gave English lessons all day long. There had been no question of a divorce; as the law stood, my father was responsible for the education of his children, but I, the seventh child, was far too young even for a kindergarten. Again, according to the law, my father did not have to pay any alimony unless compelled to do so by an order of the court, and my mother refused to go to such extremes. Thus she and I were very poor.

I think it was about 1906 when I reached my eighth year that I began thinking of the family as a many-layered cake. The top layer, particularly rich, consisted of cousins who lived in colonnaded mansions on the South Bank, the Mayfair of St Petersburg, and even in palaces. A cousin I barely knew was maid-of-honour to a Grand Duchess. Another, Madame Naryshkina, was Mistress of the Robes to the last Empress of Russia. Still another first cousin had his rooms at the Marble Palace because he was one of the A.D.C.s to Grand Duke Constantine. It was all a remote but none the less gorgeous pattern of a life at court and in guards regiments, but my father, whom I never knew, was a scientist and bio-chemistry was not exactly a road paved with gold. Moreover, there were seven of us, all much older than myself, and a fisherman on one of the lesser islands once said to me:

'The seventh child of a seventh son, are you? Why, by all the Saints, rivers of gold will flow your way some day.'

I did not quite believe him, but it was good to hear such words on a pale golden summer morning by the banks of the Chernaya, one of the Neva's tributaries. Kingcups and cuckoo flowers were spreading their embroidery at our feet. The thorn and the May tree were in full flower, and it was easy to laugh.

Below that very rich top layer was another, not so rich but much more accessible and interesting: Uncle Alexis, his family, and a wide circle of men and women of intellect, vision and attainment who frequented his home.

Below lay a most curious layer—mostly of female first cousins who married into titled families, lived either on their husbands' estates or wherever their men held important civil service posts.

They came to St Petersburg for balls, concerts and operas. Some of them paid us rare visits and vanished into splendour again. Those cousins were like gaily coloured butterflies flying over the city. No sooner had one noticed them than they flew away, leaving behind waves of delicate scent.

Below those came a sombrely coloured layer of widowed aunts whose husbands, killed in some war or other, had left them little more than memories and meagre pensions; and of retired, remote cousins who seldom came to St Petersburg because, as they said, its prices were steep and its climate abominable.

And, finally, at the very bottom was the layer to which I belonged because of our poverty, and yet from the earliest years I considered myself rich because I had St Petersburg. We lived now in one small flat, now in another, on Vassily Island—to the undisguised contempt, brushed with pity, of 'the upper layers'—but we kept servants because wages were sinfully low. Yet there was my Uncle Alexis's home and the wide circle of his friends—poets, painters, novelists, singers and members of the Imperial Ballet. He had Chekhov among the contributors to his children's monthly, *Rodnik*.

My uncle lived in an enormous flat on Zakharievskaya Street. Not a rich man, he had married a girl of wealth, and it was in their home that I saw an armchair for the first time in my life. But the elegant furnishings and the menservants meant nothing to me. There was his library, a spacious room, its four windows affording a superb view of the river, and I would be allowed to read there on condition that any book was to be put back in its place. In his life-time, however, that brilliant circle was not even names to me: I felt far too shy to leave the quiet of the library for the crowded drawing-room and dining-room.

My uncle died in 1910, and the great Chaliapin came to sing at his funeral.

Leo Tolstoy

When the traditional mourning was over, my Aunt Catherine opened her doors again, but somehow or other the library was not as accessible as it had been, and I must creep into the farthest corner of the drawing-room, there crouch on a stool, stare and listen. I remember seeing a wild-haired young man with piercing dark eyes. 'Blok is going to recite,' said someone, and I felt as though the gates of heaven were being opened to me. My uncle's daughter, Natalie, went up to the young man who bowed and got up. Not quite able to catch the sense of the poem, I was entranced by the voice. Later I would learn that people of judgment considered Alexander Blok the greatest poet since Pushkin.

I remember one evening when a letter written by Tolstoy to Natalie, lay on a table for all to look at, and she entertained the guests by her description of a visit she had paid to Yasnaya Poliana, Tolstoy's country home. The great man's younger son, Leo, was there and Anna Akhmatova with her husband, Goumilev, also a poet, Golovin the painter, and such 'giants' in the world of children's books as Zharinzova and Avenarius. Once I saw an elegant woman in deep rose velvet and a picture hat with pale ostrich feathers. The way she came in, stood talking to my aunt for a few minutes, drank a cup of tea, and went, were so many musical phrases. I watched her from my corner and thought she looked like a bird.

It was Matilda Kshesinskaya, the most famous ballerina of the day.

Those were golden occasions—in spite of my Aunt Catherine who made no secret of her contempt for 'poor relations'. I now think that she invited my mother and me in hopes that some cousins of my mother's would be cajoled to come to the gatherings. My aunt was beautiful but not clever. Her great drawing-room was a forum but she took no part in any discussion. Men and women of high intellectual and artistic quality gathered there because they had been friends of my uncle and transferred their affection to his children: Natalie, who wrote, and Boris who was rapidly making a name for himself at the Mariinsky Theatre where he painted décors for ballet and opera. The guests did not come for food, and Aunt Catherine, for all her wealth, saw to it that they got as little as possible! Tea would be offered with tiny sugared rusks and little currant buns carefully halved! The plates, once emptied, were not replenished.

Mouse-like, I kept to my corner. I knew well that my aunt seldom missed a chance to make a barbed remark and I kept out of her way as much as possible. But in 1912, I remember, a passion for ancient history swept over me. There were no free libraries in St Petersburg. One afternoon, allowed to read a book in the library, I saw a whole shelf of George Ebert's novels. All dealt with Ancient Egypt. I caught sight of Natalie and asked if I might borrow one or two. I had done it before and she knew that I treated books with the respect they deserved.

'Of course,' Natalie said kindly. 'Help yourself.'

I laid two or three books on the table when Aunt Catherine passed the open door, saw me and came into the room.

'Borrowing again! What a little sponger you are! When we come to see you, we never take anything!'

I might have said that there was nothing to be taken in our poor home, but I kept silent. I replaced the three books very carefully. I heard Natalie say that she had given me permission to borrow. My aunt shrugged and went back to the drawing-room but the Ebert novels remained on the shelf and never again did I ask for a loan.

Once the guests started a heated discussion about St Petersburg. From my corner I listened and heard most fantastically varied opinions. Some argued that the city was beautiful but too alien to win a Russian heart. Others maintained that only one season, winter, was bearable there. There fell a pause and I heard my aunt's mocking voice:

'Well, I have a niece who is quite potty about the city. Come on, Poppy, tell us what you think of it all.'

Crimson to the lobes of my ears, I slid off the stool, moved forward a little, and stood dumb. What could I say to that brilliant gathering? I clenched my hot hands and heard Aunt Catherine say:

'I know you are not at your ease in Russian. You may speak English.'

I bent my head when a woman's gentle voice came to my rescue.

'She is so young, and the young are often shy—especially about people and places they love.'

I did not dare look up. I crept back to my corner. Later Natalie asked me:

'Well, aren't you proud of having such a distinguished champion?'

'Who was she?'

'Madame Dostoyevsky.'

'Oh!' I murmured and raised my head. In the doorway an elderly woman in dark brown velvet was shaking hands with my aunt.

'There she is—just going. Come—I will introduce you.'

But I shook my head.

In spite of many unpleasantnesses, those parties did more for me than I realized at the time. My Aunt Catherine wounded my pride often enough; yet, all unwittingly she afforded endless opportunities to enrich my mind. By accident of birth I was unable to enter any free school in St Petersburg, and the fees of private establishments were wholly beyond our means. Not until 1913, more than a year after my father's death, was I accepted as a pupil at one of the so-called Nobility and Gentry boarding schools. More will be said of that oddly coloured experience later on.

And meanwhile my aunt's home remained, an enchanting corner of an enchanting city where anything exciting might happen, where, listening, I learned far more than any school could teach me. The Ebert incident must have shamed Natalie because at our next visit she had some books all ready parcelled up for me, and when I muttered that I did not wish 'to borrow', she said briskly:

'I am sure you would not like to hurt me.'

One blissful afternoon in the spring of 1911 I grew articulate. Count Leo Tolstoy, the novelist's son, and my cousin, Boris, were deep in a discussion on Italian art, Boris having just returned from Italy. They sat at a little table by a window and, having heard a few familiar names, I crept near them, my habitual shyness for once slipping off.

'The greatest among them all belongs to the world, not just to Italy,' I said.

They looked surprised, and Boris asked:

'Which of them?'

'Why, Leonardo—' and, having read quite a number of books about him, I started defending my statement until both fact and vocabulary failed me.

Count Leo smiled.

'So St Petersburg is not your only love.' He turned to Boris, 'I wonder what your little cousin will do when she is grown up and stops wearing a red bow in her hair.'

'Well, she'll never be a painter,' replied Boris. 'She needs a ruler to draw a straight line and even then manages to make it crooked.'

Toward's Vassily Island

CHAPTER THREE

Vassily Island

IT WAS anything but the Mayfair of St Petersburg. For all the beauty it offered, it was the home of socially unimportant people. Its shops catered for their modest needs and its slums gave some kind of shelter to the least blessed men and women in the city. The island was my home, school and delight for twenty years, all its curves and coils known and loved since early childhood. It was a mother, a nurse and a mistress all in one. It spoke of tenderness sometimes; then it drifted into sterner accents and taught me some of life's hardihoods. But it never cheated, and I knew I could trust all it said to me.

34

It lay on the North Bank of the Neva and was by far the biggest of the nineteen islands. Its Finnish name used to be Hares' Island. Together with Viborg Side, Vassily Island shared in the city's beginnings. The very first stone mansion to be built in St Petersburg, the home of Prince Menshikov, stood there. In my days, it was the First Military School, *Perviy Kadetzky Korpus*, and the street came to be known as *Kadetzkaya* Line. A little further to the east stood the government offices, a very long two-storied building, a beautifully-vaulted cloister bordering it from end to end. In 1819 the Emperor Alexander I founded St Petersburg University and, until its enlargement in the mid-nineteenth century, the libraries and lecture-rooms remained as they had been since 1705. The magnificent Academy of Sciences, founded by the Empress Catherine I in 1727, faced the waterfront. To the north-west Vassily Island was known as the Gavan, the very first port in St Petersburg, its western tip washed by the waters of the Gulf of Finland, and its narrow streets housing dockers, stevedores and shipwrights. Down to my time one of those streets was known as *Korabelnaya*, i.e. Ship Street. The Gavan lay low and was the first part of the island to suffer from floods which, their disastrous effects swinging like a pendulum, were a practically annual event, and even as a child I felt puzzled why all those fragile timbered houses had not been replaced by stone buildings better fitted to withstand the savage onslaught of swollen waters. The very first flood I remember happened in deep autumn in 1903. Looking out of a window I saw boats plying up and down the wide street.

'It can't be the Neva!' I cried to my nurse because the deep blue clear water I had already learned to love was a muddy coffee-coloured mess, tinged here and there with irregular patches of dirty grey-white.

Then in 1909, I think, when we lived in the 9th Line, the

great courtyard was covered with water and we all woke in the night, the crash of the smashed double gates suggesting the roar of several cannon. All the tenants on the ground and first floors were moved into safety. The tragedy linked the entire population of the vast house into one compact unit. A committee was formed and that within an hour, in a top floor flat. Food supplies were listed, not a single tenant objecting to the inspection of his or her larder. I still remember our fat cook from the neighbourhood of Reval counting what potatoes, onions and carrots she had in her kitchen. The shortage of water, however, presented difficulties the committee could not meet. It was the yard porter and his mate who, up to their knees in water, contrived to make a clumsy raft, had several empty wooden tubs tied to it and ventured towards the eastern end of the island still beyond the reach of the flood. They brought the raft back, all the tubs filled with clean water. It was a heroic feat and the men were fittingly rewarded.

Yet those were but minor discomforts when compared with the tragedy of the poor Gavan where hundreds of timbered houses were smashed. The actual number of casualties never came to light. The marine police sent boats to rescue the dispossessed folk, who were all taken to the Cadet School where women of the neighbourhood happily spared the ravages, peeled off their sodden clothes and plied them with hot drinks and soup. A municipal relief unit braved the wrath of the Neva and reached the Cadet School bringing more clothes and food. When, after four or five days, the waters fell back, many people from the South Bank opened their great mansions to the refugees and the merchants lost no time in starting a relief fund. Yet, as I thought, however vaguely, no gift of money or clothing could make it really easier for so many widows and orphans or restore all those shattered homes. All of it seemed both wrong and unnecessary. The fathers of the city should have made it their business to make the Gavan and other low-lying islands secure from the onslaught of the sea. Once only did I allow myself to be articulate but Boris, my cousin, never saw my point.

'If it comes to that, Peter the Great should never have founded St Petersburg,' he said, and I disagreed most vehemently.

*

Nicholas Bridge to the west and Palace Bridge to the east linked Vassily Island with the South Side where I was born and where we should have gone on living if the iron compulsion of financial straits had not driven us across the river when I was about two years old and what riches came to me when the mind and the imagination, to say nothing of the heart, acknowledged the Island to be a true home!

Its waterfront was superb with the great massif of the Stock Exchange, the honey-coloured buildings of the University, the dark green splash of Roumiantzev Garden, the severe grey beauty of the Academy of Sciences, the Zoological Museum, and the Academy of Arts, its walls brilliant with mosaics. University Quay ended there, giving place to Nicholas Quay with its row of shops, some private houses, the great pale buildings of the Imperial Naval College and, finally, the enormous Institute of Mines. Starting with the latter, right down to Nicholas Bridge, the quayside throbbed with life from the end of April until October when foreign ships had no choice but to weigh anchor and start on their homeward voyage because the Gulf froze hard during the winter. During the summer months that stretch of the quayside was far more interesting and exciting than any geography book: the whistling winches, the ceaseless concert of sea-gulls, the shouts of crews come from every corner of the globe, the lusty singing of Russian and

Finnish stevedores, and the avalanche of most varied cargoes spilling out of the holds. . . . Even on a comparatively quiet day, the wind would ride high and, however wide the quay-side, you had to pick your way in among crates, bags and bundles of every conceivable shape and size. On a sunny day, the latticed lids of some crates gleamed seductively, oranges and lemons adding their share of colour to the multicoloured scene.

Viewed from a high belfry, Vassily Island suggested a quilt, its twenty-six Lines interspersed by three equally wide Boulevards: *Bolshoy* (Big), nearest to the quayside; *Sredny* (Middle); and *Maly* (Little), its sluminess facing one of the Neva's four tributaries, the Little Neva. The predominant colour through spring and summer was green, trees being planted along the Lines and Boulevards. In the autumn, the Island was well-nigh drowned in deep gold and bronze.

The South Bank inhabitants were apt to consider Vassily Island as something beyond the pale. It certainly had no important shops, and its rents and rates were low. Even so, it had sharply drawn social distinctions. From Kadetzkaya down to the 5th Line it carried a faintly well-bred air. That vanished with the 6th Line and its neighbour, the 7th, which was noisily and shamelessly commercial. From the 8th Line down to the 14th the Island was quite frankly middle-class. Beyond, right on the Gavan, stood row upon row of tenement houses divided into cheap flats of two or three small rooms and terraces inhabited by those who could not afford even the smallest flat and lived in one room, sharing a communal kitchen and other amenities.

The same distinction applied to the three Boulevards. *Bolshoy* was eminently respectable at its eastern end; *Sredny* was just 'possible' except for the dinginess of its shops, and *Maly* was quite obviously a slum.

The Island's most important sanctuary stood on the 6th Line —St Andrew's Cathedral, and close to it, cleaving its way almost into the heart of the 5th Line spread St Andrew's Market held on every day of the year. It seemed something of a mercantile extension to the severely orthodox piety of the Cathedral. The narrow lanes between the stalls teemed with shoppers, onlookers, pedlars and, inevitably, the beggars who hoped to be more fortunate there than near the Cathedral porch. The whining 'an alms for Christ's sake' was all too often drowned by pedlars shouting their wares and stallholders extolling the quality of their stock to the level of sheer fantasy.

'Come on folks, here are apples better than the Tzar eats!'

'Princes and counts could not have such fine veal served at their tables! Just melts in your mouth, it does.'

'Now here are shoes all handsewn! They will carry you to Kiev and back again and be none the worse for it, St Andrew be my witness!'

'Ten copeks for this little saucepan, and it will serve you twenty years!'

No shopper ever paid the price asked for. 'Two copeks for this cabbage! I would not have it for nothing—'

'Fifteen copeks for such a water melon? Are you making fun of me? Eight would be too much.'

Sometimes stallholders would shake their heads and call on the whole heavenly hierarchy to witness their honesty, but more often than not they would say:

'Ah well! Have it your way—as the saying goes, if ruin comes, no use kicking against it.'

The market sold practically everything: food, ironmongery, cheap clothing and shoes, crockery. A few stalls were heaped with second-hand junk from cracked shellframed mirrors to white satin shoes sadly down at heel.

I think I was about ten when I found myself in frightful trouble at St Andrew's Market. Our cook, armed with two huge baskets, used to go there three or four times a week and occasionally I was allowed to join her. Now St Andrew's teemed with pedlars who hawked most appetizing wares: piping hot patties, apples baked in honey, and *baranki*, a kind of circular cracknel thickly coated with poppy seeds. It happened on a particularly cold but sunny November day. Our cook began chaffering with a butcher when I saw a pedlar whose big wooden tray carried nothing but patties—mushroom, egg, fish and jam. I had not a copper in my pockets, but I knew the cook had some money. I looked at the tray and knew I was hungry. I chose three patties. The young man handed them over on a clean white plate. I was well aware of the custom: the plate must be given back, the money lying on it.

The patties being rather small, it did not take me long to eat them, and I handed the plate back.

'Nine copeks—' said the young man.

I looked towards the butcher's stall. Our cook had gone.

'Nine copeks—' he repeated impatiently.

I dashed forward to find the cook but could not see her anywhere. The pedlar ran and seized me by the elbow.

'Pay me at once,' he hissed, 'or else I call for a policeman. . . .'

I looked up and down the long narrow lane, but the familiar green and yellow headscarf was nowhere to be seen. Terrified almost to the point of tears and thoroughly ashamed, I tried to explain, but the pedlar would not listen. He whistled, still clutching my elbow, and all too soon a portly, bearded policeman came up. By then my voice had gone. The pedlar told the story briefly and honestly: I had asked for three patties, eaten them and had no money to pay. I owed him nine copeks.

The fat policeman whisked out an extremely dirty notebook and a stump of a pencil. Slowly, laboriously he wrote down everything told him by the pedlar, and then asked for details which—even in my confusion, I thought to be quite unnecessary:

'What kind of patties did she have?'

'Mushroom, egg and apple.'

'Ah—' said the policeman and bent over the notebook again.

'They were all the same price—' ventured the pedlar, and the policeman bridled up.

'You speak when you are spoken to, my son!' and he turned to me: 'Name and address, and be quick about it.'

Gulping and stammering, I gave the name and address. The former made him frown. The latter made him purse his lips.

'You live with your mother, you say? Is she a dressmaker, or a baker's wife?'

Here, to my relief, our cook appeared.

'My mistress a dressmaker? A baker's wife? That is a good one! You wait and I am going to tell the sergeant about it, and her Excellency too!'

In a flash the pedlar and I changed parts. He was the criminal, daring to accuse her Excellency's daughter of a petty theft! The policeman swore, using words I could not understand, and then kicked him so hard that the great wooden tray fell down on the dirty trampled snow. All shame and horror forgotten, I flamed with anger and stamped my foot.

'But I do owe him money,' I shouted at the policeman, and our cook produced the needed coins. The pedlar was paid, the policeman slouched off, and the cook scolded me.

'Hasn't the mistress told you ever so many times never to buy anything from a pedlar?'

I did not listen. I had forgotten the pedlar. I knew I would never forget the policeman and the nauseating change in his manner on being told who my mother was. For some time I avoided St Andrew's Market.

★

I remember Vassily if most vividly because of Amos and

Obadiah, two red spaniels who belonged to the Island as much as the Island belonged to them. They lived in a big house on Nicholas Quay, and they were owned (though common gossip had it that they owned him) by an odd-looking old bachelor born in St Petersburg of English parents. People said that he knew no English. He kept a carriage and horse. Summer and winter he wore a funny round fur cap trimmed with yellow plush. He was seen very seldom, but clocks and watches could be set by Amos and Obadiah.

Every morning they set out, always beautifully groomed, the brass studs on their collars shining like gold. They walked side by side, with an air of owning the very pavement under their feet. If some mongrel or even a respectably-bred dog tried either to make friends or to start a fight, Amos growled ferociously and Obadiah would be ready to spring. If some sentimental female stopped and started to exclaim, 'Oh, you lovely pets,' the contempt in their eyes beggared all description.

They roamed all over Vassily Island until our yard porter said it should be christened Spaniels' Island. But they also wandered much further afield and would cross Nicholas Bridge, walking over to St Isaac's Cathedral by way of the interminable Horse-Guards Boulevard. Once I met them resting under a lilac bush in the Summer Gardens, and one lovely June morning I came on them playing some mysterious game of their own in the shady Alexander Gardens behind the Admiralty on the South Side. Sometimes they allowed me to stroke their silken heads, though their manner suggested that such a liberty should not be taken too often.

They were never seen engaged in an unseemly brawl and must have been twin exemplars to every dog-owner in St Petersburg. Then they blotted their escutcheon most disgracefully. . . .

We heard the story from our cook, very proud of having been an eye-witness. She was on her way to St Andrew's

Market when she heard loud shouting and saw Amos and Obadiah running as swift as lightning, a huge juicy joint in Obadiah's mouth. A good distance behind ran a butcher's boy in his blue-and-white-striped apron, his face scarlet, and his right arm brandishing a long piece of thick rope.

But he could not catch up with Amos and Obadiah, and onlookers either took it all as a joke or else retreated at the first deep growl from Amos. Down the 7th Line they flew, turned right to Nicholas Quay, and reached their home. Presumably they shared the loot in some corner of the big yard.

'How plucky of them!' I said, but my mother thought otherwise.

'How very stupid of them! They are far too well known, and the butcher won't leave it at that. . . .'

The butcher did not. To steal as expensive a joint as a saddle of mutton, already paid for by a valued customer, was a crime of no mean order. The old man in the funny cap paid for the joint and for the damage to the boy's trousers caused by a fall during the chase. But Amos and Obadiah had to face their punishment. They roamed about in the great yard of the house, but its gates were shut and the porter would not let them out. On rare occasions they went out with their master in the open carriage, but there were leads to their collars. I heard it said that they went as far as Petrovsky Park on one of the outlying islands where the leads would be taken off and the spaniels were free to run about, but I wondered if they ever enjoyed themselves again. I thought that the theft of a joint was nothing but a mischievous prank—they were too well fed ever to scrounge for food.

Seen no longer, Amos and Obadiah were never forgotten, and for quite a time the Island wore an orphaned look.

★

Vassily Island belonged to the beginnings of St Petersburg and it taught me history. The great river running down to the sea owned it as much as its blue waters were owned by it. The dark green splash of its trees was at once a welcome and a challenge.

Our first home there was in a big flat in a house on the 4th Line. There followed two or three moves, and the very last steading was not even a flat but two rooms at the least respectable end of Bolshoy Boulevard. The rooms were on the sixth floor; there was a lift worked by a sour middle-aged woman who grumbled about the weather all through the four seasons and bewailed the high price of butter and herrings. We could not afford to tip her very often and her grievances grew in volume. Yet she belonged to Vassily Island, and so did I.

Bolshoy Boulevard, whatever its social gradations, was lovely from end to end because of its trees and its nearness to the great river. Sredny Boulevard brushed close to slumminess and many shops were dirty, particularly butchers and fishmongers. Its dusty yards smelt. We bought neither meat nor fish there but, surprisingly enough, Sredny had quite a few decent grocers and bakers. Its shoeshops were good and cheap, but none of our servants liked shopping there. Pickpockets sprang up like mushrooms after a rainy night and some were bold enough to snatch a handbag or a shopping basket. The shout 'stop the thief' sometimes produced a policeman, but the public seemed oddly indifferent. In the summer, many of the food shops displayed their goods outside. A boy or an old woman would keep guard, seated on an empty barrel. Yet some of them made rather odd guardians. There were cases when some among them brought an empty sack, 'just for comfort', would spread it over the lid of the barrel and slip now one article, now another into it. When closing time came, 'the guardians' would most virtuously help in carrying the goods inside the shop, linger about until the shutters were up, and then slink back to the barrel, fill the sack, and steal away, the very poor lighting along Sredny much to their advantage.

Yet the Boulevard did not lack pretensions. It boasted two of the very first cinemas on the Island. One, called 'Tip Top', was the first I visited, in 1909, I think. The film given was *Don Quixote*, and I went home angry with myself for having wasted four copeks. I knew my Cervantes too well to reconcile the gaudy film to the great classic.

Maly Boulevard was slummy to the degree of abandon, though its slumminess was somewhat redeemed at its northern end by its nearness to the estuary. The houses, most of them ochre-coloured, looked as wizened as old men from the work-house. The shops had small grimy windows where suspiciously pink sausages were neighboured by balls of string, bunches of nails, necklaces of dusty dried mushrooms, besoms and bags of most vividly coloured fruitdrops called *ledenzy*. Some of the houses sported gaudy curtains and notices of 'Rooms to let'. Maly had no restaurants but there were many *chaynaya*, tea-rooms where the very poor could get a kettle of hot water for nothing and those slightly better-off could quieten their hunger by pickled eels, fried potatoes and a sausage for five copeks, with a glass of tea thrown in. Maly had many pubs, *traktyrs*, their interior unknown to me. Workmen, small bottles of vodka in their hands, would come out, break the seal and then and there empty the bottle in one or two gulps. There were also curious second-hand clothes shops, most of the tattered stock spread out on the pavement and guarded by shabby fat women, greed and cunning in their eyes.

Maly was out of bounds to me, and I was nearly thirteen when I first discovered it. It was certainly grim, but it was bone of the Island's bone and flesh of its flesh, and I felt that I must learn something of its penury and squalor. There were houses where a room would be divided into so many 'corners', but in the summer people amused themselves in the open air, dancing, playing the accordion, cracking sunflower seeds which cost a farthing a pound, and drinking tea out of chipped mugs. Here and there one could come on evidences of violence, largely caused by the people's passion for vodka, but in general the people both there and along the streets and alleys of the Gavan thought no more of their penury than of last winter's snow.

I remember a quaint baker's shop owned by a fat and glossy German. It stood on the ground floor of a timbered house with much carving over the windows and the eaves. It had a gabled roof. Hanging on the door was a notice pencilled in bright red, every word most funnily mis-spelt: 'Credit not allowed. Do not come in unless you can pay.' I have no idea how the fat German earned a livelihood: no matter how often I passed by, I never saw anyone either going in or coming out. But the little house may well have been occupied by some Dutch or German shipwright in the days of Peter the Great: two of the first floor windows had carvings of little boats under their sills.

My favourite short wander was down the waterfront from Nicholas Quay, past the University gateway, to where a giant statue of Neptune guarded the eastern tip of the Island. There was very little traffic in those days; on clear afternoons throughout all the seasons the South Bank gleamed pearl and golden, and the exquisite spire of the Admiralty looked as though it were built of magic. In the summer you could hear the plashing of water against stone and lose yourself in the beauty both shaped and unshaped by man. The great river had run its course long, long before the names of Swede, Finn and Russian entered History, and it ran wholly indifferent to all the changes on land contrived by man. It imposed its will on the great buildings along the quays of Vassily Island, the tattered scene of Maly, and on the scented drawing-rooms of Palace Quay across on the South Bank. The sea and the river made Vassily Island a good place to grow up in even though the address made some of my relations wonder how we could 'bear' it. I enjoyed it all to the utmost, and I remember all its gifts with gratitude.

CHAPTER FOUR

St Petersburg's Ghosts and Mysteries

THE CITY easily lent herself both to legendary ghost stories and what might be called a supernatural reality. The soft colours, the incessant orchestra of the waters, the secretive shadows under old elms and limes in her many pleasances, all of it produced an atmosphere in which, as it were, one could and did expect the unexpected.

Yet that atmosphere did not reflect one unbroken entity. The nineteen islands had once belonged to Scandinavia and the northern folklore struck deep roots. Then they became the capital of Russia, clothed with a new identity, as it were, and the latter shaped legends and superstitions of its own. Finally and inevitably, St Petersburg, for all her Scandinavian and Finnish elements, came to absorb much of the purely Russian folklore. The three streams did not run along completely separate courses. They kept threading into one another and often enough some fragment of Finnish or Swedish folklore brushed against something known to the Slavs.

When, at the age of seven or eight, I went to Finland to stay with my Danish grandmother, I did not find it difficult to follow the counsels of her Finnish housekeeper since those fragments of northern folklore were well known to me. For instance, when I found a clump of wild strawberries in one of the parks in St Petersburg, I knew that I must be careful and leave a few berries untouched because 'the little folk ran about so much that they often lost their shoe-buttons and needed the berries for more and more buttons'. White lilac was never to be brought into the house because the tiny folk used it for their caps and bonnets. It was unlucky to carry an acorn in your pocket: for all you knew, a tiny gentleman was defrauded of a tankard. The cushions of multicoloured moss, which grew in St Petersburg, were really so many mattresses, rugs and blankets for the use of the fairy world inhabitants. Apparently my grandmother thought nothing of filling big bowls with them—much to her housekeeper's anguish. If I came on a uniformly coloured pebble by the lake shore or on a river bank, it was quite safe to pick it up, but if the pebble were veined, it was to be left untouched because that kind was used by the little folk for building their houses.

Such, then, were a few elements of northern folklore that St Petersburg accepted for her own. The ancient Russian superstitions, so far as I can remember, did not deal with 'little people'. If you met a monk or a black cat in a street, you either stood still or turned back home—to avoid disaster falling on you. If you put on any garment inside out, you would court illness and even death by changing it. If you dreamt about fog or a piece of water, you were certain to meet with some unpleasantness during the day unless you swallowed a pinch of salt before breakfast. If a mouse or a spider were seen in daytime, a sign of the cross had to be made at once to avoid the malice of the devil. If a young bird alighted on your windowsill, you had to stop whatever you were doing and keep still until it flew away. That assured good fortune for three weeks and three days.

Such things were far more difficult to observe than the old Norse customs. If you turned back every time you met a monk or a black cat in St Petersburg, you would never have got anywhere at all. The only time I remember seeing a young sparrow perch on the window-sill was a day in April 1910; I at once put down my pen and kept still until the bird had flown off. My 'good fortune' broke upon me in a singular fashion: the same day my mother and I lunched with the head of the family, my first cousin, Alexander. I moved my right hand rather clumsily and an exquisite Dresden coffee cup fell off the table on to the parquet floor. My cousin's wife was so painfully polite about it that I felt like a worm.

Yet some of the customs, whatever their origin, were most rewardingly impersonal. They brought neither good fortune nor ill luck. They were just beautiful. For instance, on Trinity Sunday all the nineteen islands were wreathed most luxuriantly in boughs of young birch, *berezka*. The custom, sanctified by the church, went far back to pagan days when whole birch trees used to be carried in processions in honour of Perun, the Jupiter of the Slav Olympus.

*

Again St Petersburg, for all she was young among cities, created her own legends and ghosts.

In the centre of them all stood Peter the Great. The poet
Pushkin in his *Bronze Rider* told the story of the Emperor leaping off the granite pedestal in the Senate Square and galloping
all over the city during the great flood of 1824. But the legend
went much further back than that. Many people did not believe

that Peter died in 1725. They were convinced he lay asleep under the white marble sarcophagus in the Cathedral of SS. Peter and Paul, the mausoleum of the Romanov dynasty on the North Bank of the Neva. When any danger threatened the city, Peter would wake up, lift the lid of the sarcophagus, and come out. In my childhood I met people who were certain of having seen the Emperor cross the Trinity Bridge, turn sharp to the right, reach the Summer Gardens, and then vanish. There was at least one story about him which I found hard to disbelieve because one of my brothers was involved in it.

All the members of the Imperial family lay in state at SS. Peter and Paul for three days and three nights before the funeral. Now, it used to be a custom in Russia not to put the coffin lid down until after the very last religious offices were over. Tsars, Grand-Dukes and their wives would lie, a purple velvet coverlet over them just up to the shoulders. The regalia would be arranged at the head of the coffin placed on a high trestle draped with black and gold brocade. For three days and three nights a specially chosen guard of honour kept motionless watch at the four corners of the trestle. In 1908 the Lord High Admiral of the Fleet, Grand-Duke Alexis, uncle of the last Emperor Nicholas II, died abroad, and his body was brought to St Petersburg. The guard of honour were young men from the Naval College, and my brother went on duty the third and last night. They took their places and bent their heads. The Cathedral was sunk in deep shadows, faintly broken here and there by the flickering candles.

Suddenly, a wave of icy cold swept down the nave. Quite involuntarily the young men raised their heads. From behind a pillar came a sound of steel clanging against stone and the cold grew so intense that the young men's teeth chattered. In the candlelight they saw a giant of a man in full armour, the imperial mantle thrown over the left shoulder. He approached the trestle, mounted the three steps, bent over the Grand-Duke and kissed his forehead. Nobody remembered what happened later except that the iciness vanished. Nobody saw the figure disappear into the shadows. When the relief came, the four young men left the Cathedral, their faces as white as chalk.

I did not disbelieve the story, but I felt that the founder of St Petersburg might have chosen a different moment and a less frightening manner to say goodbye to a Romanov.

A successor of Peter the Great, the Emperor Paul I (1796–1801) left an even more horrifying story.

What I knew as the Sappers' College had once been called St Michael's Castle. He built it and there, one March night in 1801, he was strangled in his bedroom and no Romanov ever lived there again. But Paul's ghost would not forsake it. Cruel, selfish and bad-tempered in the flesh, Paul was even more unpleasing as a ghost. He was supposed to roam from one room to another, his distorted face covered by a piece of white linen. Now and again his shrill voice could be heard snarling and cursing his murderers. He loved smashing furniture, particularly mirrors, and sometimes the piece of white linen which covered his face would be reinforced by a shroud falling down to the ankles. Mercifully, Paul's activities went no further than St Michael's Castle: he was never seen haunting the Cathedral where his tomb was, or the Winter Palace.

I believe that when the castle was turned into the Sappers' College, Paul's private apartments were wholly demolished, the workmen refusing to do their job except by daylight.

Yet not all the ghosts of St Petersburg were as horrifying. . . .

A sister of the head of the family, Sophia, one of the most accessible and lovable cousins I had, was married to an officer in the Cavalry Guards, and they had a flat on the third floor of an early nineteenth-century house in the aristocratic Sergyievskaya Street. Just below, on the second floor landing, was a heavily padlocked door. It led into a flat 'not to be let'. The rents were high, and my cousin made inquiries. The hall porter, *shweizar*, as they used to be called, said he had not been there long enough to know anything. The *dvornik*, or yard porter, looked ill at ease and muttered that it was best not to speak of such things. At last, Sophia came on a story as told her by a garrulous dressmaker in the neighbourhood.

That flat was haunted. It would be let time and time again, and on every occasion the tenant broke the lease. 'But what is the ghost?' insisted my cousin. The little dressmaker shuddered. 'Why, Madam, I have heard folk say it is something terrible and it jumps on you.'

Sophia waited for her husband to get back from his regimental manœuvres in the environs of St Petersburg. Like her, he was deeply interested in ghosts and they made a plan together. One autumn night when all the servants were safely asleep, they slipped downstairs, my cousin carrying a basket with a candle, some matches, a bottle of wine and sandwiches. On second thoughts she put her small golden baptismal cross on top of the basket. Her husband managed to force the padlock without much effort and they went in, closing the door behind them.

The flat was unfurnished, and it had not been lived in for a long time. It should have been dusty and musty. It was not, and it gave them the sense of being lived in and cared for. Sophia lit the candle. No monsters leaped at them from any corner. They groped their way to a broad marble window-sill, sat down and waited in silence. Presently, they were aware of a delicate fragance in the room—'just as though there were violets near us.—' my cousin said afterwards.

They kept very still, and each was conscious of a happiness surrounding them. There came a very faint rustle as if a woman were shaking her silken skirts and an echo or two of

young and happy laughter. They peered and saw nothing. The
windows were shuttered, and the light of the candle did not
betray them.

The fragance now receded, then came nearer. At last faint
whispers reached them. They distinguished the words: 'Oh, I
am so happy,' and a young man's voice whispering, 'Oh how
I love you!' Presently they saw something like a cloud at the
opposite end of the room. Within that cloud moved a young
woman's figure dressed in pale lilac. A young man in a blue
coat and fawn pantaloons stood close by. Their hands were
clasped together and Sophia saw the gleam of a wedding ring.
Then the cloud thickened, the figures vanished. Nothing remained except a delicate scent and a sense of happiness all round
about them.

'I could have sat on that window-sill for ever—' said Sophia
afterwards.

They went back upstairs (the wine undrunk and the sandwiches uneaten), having thoughtfully provided a new padlock
in place of the one they had broken. In their own drawing-
room they compared notes. Both had seen and felt exactly the
same.

A little later Sophia and her husband had to leave for the
Caucasus. I, knowing the story, would sometimes walk down
that street and stare at the shuttered windows on the second
floor. My cousin was well known for her truthfulness. In my
own mind I christened the flat 'an arbour of laughter'. Nobody
believed it. I can only suppose that all the tenants were sour-
minded folk, unwilling to allow happiness to others. So, perhaps, that dressmaker's 'monster' did leap at them. I could never
tell.

On Petersburg Side, an island on the North Bank of the Neva,
stood an ugly church built in the days of the Empress Elizabeth
(1741–1761). Its belfry seemed rather drunken, all but leaning

against the trunk of an old elm. The belfry was declared unsafe, but nobody thought of demolishing it and people were summoned to services by two hand-bells most untunefully shaken by the deacon and the clerk. Yet on four days in the year, Easter, Trinity Sunday, Michaelmas and Epiphany, the belfry came to life. The door leading to it was barred and bolted from top to bottom. The bells rang true but rather low and plaintive. We lived on St Petersburg Side through the summer of 1909, and in the evening of Trinity Sunday my mother and I were in the small but pleasant gardens adjoining the church. She was reading *Rob Roy* to me, and I was lost in the story when the bells broke out. My mother closed the book at once and said that someone must have broken down the door to the belfry.

'The church will be empty now,' she said, 'I'd better tell a policeman.'

It took us quite a time to find one. I thought that his bearded face reflected pity as he listened to my mother, whose Russian was never very fluent.

'Why, bless you, Madam,' he said when she had done. 'Nobody would dream of breaking into the belfry—that unsafe it is.'

'But the bells. . . .' she insisted, and he smiled.

'Well, I reckon the old bellmakers can come down from heaven sometimes. Four times a year they do, Madam. You will hear those bells again come Michaelmas.'

We left Petersburg Side sometime before September and I never heard the bells again. I somehow think my mother did not quite believe the bearded policeman.

But she certainly had evidence of a poltergeist's pranks.

Even on Vassily Island where rents were low, the flats fronting the quays were expensive. In the summer of 1906 we had to move because of the house being demolished. Walking down Nicholas Quay, I saw squares of white paper on the windows of a third floor flat in a house at the corner of the 14th Line. In Russia, such squares of white paper told the outside world that the flat was vacant.

I got very excited, but my mother shook her head. The rent would be beyond her, she said. Yet, on making inquiries from the hall porter, she learned that the rent was absurdly low and at once paid the deposit. We moved in—to my joy. The view was exquisite. Straight ahead ran the Neva. Beyond were the palatial mansions along the English Quay on the South Side. To the right, the queenly river widened towards the New Port. Far beyond lay the estuary and on very clear days you could see the slate-grey waters of the Gulf of Finland gleaming in the sun. Wherever you looked, you saw water and ships, ships, ships. I could not have imagined such happiness.

Winter closed in, and green-silver ice sheathed the great river. The ships were long since gone but the beauty remained.

One evening my mother sat sewing in the little sitting-room adjoining my bedroom. I had gone to bed. Suddenly she was startled by a loud crash from my room. A second later, another, and yet another.

She at once tip-toed into the room. By the light of a shaded candle she saw me fast asleep in my narrow bed. But the heavy jug from the washstand lay all shattered on the floor, and little rills of water ran everywhere. The small writing-table was overturned, the inkstand upset, and a curtain torn off its rod.

I woke up next morning in a makeshift bed in my mother's room. I can't now remember the reasons given for the change, nor was I told why my own bed and other belongings were later moved into the only spare room in the flat, but I well remember my grief when, at the end of the year, my mother decided to move, telling me that the flat was rather damp. Not till years later did I learn the truth. Apparently, that poltergeist confined his destructive activities to one room only—but every-body, myself excepted, knew of him. That explained the low rent. That also explained the frequent change of servants. I think my mother had no fewer than seven cooks during that time, and one young maid, a peasant straight from the country, left within a week.

*

Nobody could belong to St Petersburg without being aware of 'things that walked by night'. Some of the islands had been poor fishing hamlets before the days of Peter the Great. People who sailed and rowed up and down the lesser waters of the city insisted that they heard Finnish songs reaching them from some small uninhabited island or even out of the middle of the river. St Petersburg may well have been the youngest capital in the world, but she was built on the islands, their past stretching further back than recorded history, and as I grew older I came to understand—however faintly—that very peculiar vein of something like tenderness in most of those stories. Ghosts appeared to evoke long forgotten stories of shining courage, staunch loyalty and deep love. Thus, years later, a young man at the University told me that, as a boy in his teens, he and his father had stood one wintry afternoon at the northern tip of Vassily Island and saw as if in a mist the end of the great battle between Alexander, Prince of Novgorod, and a Swedish host in the early thirteenth century.

'We did see it. We heard the clang of swords and the neighing of horses. We caught a glimpse of Alexander's helmet. We did not feel a bit frightened. It seemed just like stepping from one dimension into another—quite unfamiliar, but compelling and beautiful. I suppose it lasted a few seconds. To me, it was an eternity—to see Prince Alexander's courage enfleshed again.'

Yet there were many dark corners in the city, and some of them left their imprint in a ghostly fashion.

Only the very rich had their own houses, called *osobniak*. Even the well-to-do preferred to live in flats. On Moyka Quay stood one such *osobniak*, beautifully built of pale grey stone, with a pillared porch and semi-circular steps leading to an exquisite front door. But all its windows were blind; its wrought-iron gates were closed and nobody had crossed its threshold for many a year. In my endless walks all over the city, I discovered that house, and for a reason I could not understand, its appearance frightened me. It was like a face with not a single trace of hope on it. At first I wondered whether it was due to the house standing near to Litovsky Castle, the dreaded prison of old St Petersburg. Then I knew I was wrong: there were other houses even closer to the Litovsky, and they were all ordinary and comfortable, with gay curtains to their windows, and children's laughter coming from the back gardens.

Many a time would I pass that particular house and hurry on, and not till much later did I learn its story. A double murder had once been committed there, and the murderer was never caught. But, as a woman in a neighbouring grocer's shop told me, the man died when his time came. People believed that his ghost returned to the place of his crime.

'Most nights,' said the grocer's wife, 'you hear such wailing going on there! Enough to make your blood freeze! Who could ever live there, I ask you? And what a waste,' she sighed, 'such a beautiful house! Shame I call it—'

I agreed that it was indeed beautiful.

In March 1917 the Litovsky Castle, all the prisoners released, was set on fire by the revolutionaries. It happened on a particularly wild night, and the hungry flames lost little time in reaching the forlorn *osobniak*. Nobody dreamt of fighting that fire.

My very last home in Russia happened to be on Moyka Quay. From a window I could see the blackened skeleton of that *osobniak* and I felt that whatever had once haunted it was laid to rest in its ashes.

★

So much for ghosts. But this city also had many a mystery which offered no clue.

Petrovsky Park was at quite a distance from my home, and I could not get there unless I had enough coppers for the fare on board one of the small steamers which plied up and down the Neva.

The park was laid out in the middle of the eighteenth century, and on my very first visit there in the summer of 1907 I stumbled on a most tantalizing puzzle.

At the eastern end, a big slab of purple veined Finnish granite was set up between two old birches. It was not a grave stone. Surrounded by rather clumsily chiselled laurel leaves ran the words: 'In memory of our happiest day, 20th June 1840'. Neither names nor initials were added.

At once I began looking for a keeper. The man I found was extremely polite, but he could not help me. He knew nothing about the stone and he doubted if anyone did.

'There is not a trace of any lichen on it,' I said, 'someone must be looking after it.'

'Of course we do. It is a monument, Miss, and it is our job to look after it.'

'Does anyone ever come to see it?'

'I have been here thirty-odd years, Miss. I suppose many folks pass it by and stare at it, but you are the first to ask questions about it.'

The stone remained a mystery. But my imagination would not rest. They must have been people of substance to erect such an important memorial, but who were they, and what were they? Nobody, not even my Uncle Alexis, could tell me. As I grew older, I took to searching for a clue at the Imperial Library on Nevsky Prospect, and I found nothing at all. But June was one of the loveliest months in St Petersburg, and it seemed good to think that someone had been very happy there in 1840.

It was during the same summer of 1907 that I stumbled on another mystery, this time on Vassily Island. Its very wide, tree-edged streets went by the unimaginative name of Lines. In one of them, not too far from the slumminess of Maly Boulevard, stood a very ugly church with a bright blue cupola and a startlingly green roof, a big and untidy graveyard encircling it. There I found the Chinaman's grave.

The very long stone slab set out all his Chinese names in Russian characters, the date of his coming to Russia and the date of his baptism were quite illegible, and so was the date of his death. All the rest was clear enough—the honours held in China and his rank at the Emperor's court. At the very foot of the grave were the words: 'This stone was laid by his inconsolable wife, Maria, an Esthonian peasant and a true Christian'.

Here was enough matter for a novel! A Chinaman of so exalted a position in his home-land going to Russia, settling there, marrying an Esthonian peasant, and being buried in the neighbourhood of a slum! It did not seem to make sense but, the lack of dates notwithstanding, it was History. And once again all my inquiries came to a dead end. The parish priest said there was no mention of any Chinaman in the register. 'But of course, he was a Christian to be buried here.' The parish clerk shrugged and muttered that an old grave was no concern of his, and both men thought I was a rather foolishly curious little girl given to wasting people's time with irrelevant questions.

There must have been no end to odd and mysterious touches

in the life of St Petersburg, and the last of them that I would like to remember is the box shop, which I called 'the voice shop'. Squeezed in between Konradi's chocolate shop and a stationer's, it faced Nicholas Bridge and was one of the many delights of Vassily Island, the pleasure enhanced by the mystery: no customer ever saw the proprietor. People got to know him by his voice—well modulated with that peculiar St Petersburg note in it which made anyone, say from Moscow, call it 'foreign'. But the name over the door was Russian enough! *Povarov*—meaning 'cook'.

The single window was far too small for an adequate display. You had to go down three steps to find yourself in that tiny enchanting kingdom. There were boxes of all sizes, small and big, round, square, oblong, made of rare Crimean and Caucasian woods, of birch and chestnut, apple and pear, plain and inlaid. They were set out from floor to ceiling all round the three walls, and to the left of the door stood a table crowded with exquisitely painted wooden oranges, apples, pears, even vegetables, cats and dogs, monkeys and bears, and tiny workboxes for small girls about to learn how to hem a handkerchief.

It was late spring of 1906 when I first went into that shop. A cousin, whom I did not know at all and who lived far in the South, was getting married, and one morning my Aunt Catherine paid us one of her infrequent calls. She sat for about twenty minutes and then announced that she must get a cab and be driven to Nevsky Prospect.

'Nadine's future husband is so wealthy that I must send her a really good wedding present. I think I could find something at Alexandre's.'

'Why don't you go to Povarov's?' suggested my mother. 'I have seen some of his boxes. They are exquisite.'

'I know and expensive too,' retorted my aunt. 'I got a workbox for Natalie last Christmas there. It cost the earth.'

But in the end she decided she would go to the box shop and suggested that I might come with her.

The little place was quite empty. From somewhere at the back a pleasant voice wished us the time of day.

I stood about and stared in delight, extremely pleased that my Aunt Catherine took quite a time to make up her mind. In the end she chose a jewellery box made of some glossy chestnut-coloured wood, inlaid all over with tiny honey-coloured stars and deep blue and crimson flowers. It was lined with dark violet velvet. Its price made me gasp—ten roubles. I turned to the little table to the left of the door, realizing that my pocket money was precisely twenty copeks a month and that it would have taken me an eternity to pay for some such box; but my aunt evidently thought she had stumbled on a bargain. She took the box and the money and put both on the little ledge. Through the opening a huge hairy hand came out. We heard the rustling of paper, and the pleasant voice commented on the mildness of the wind.

Out on the quay, whilst my aunt waited for a cab to take her home, I asked:

'Why didn't he come out?'

'I believe he never does. I can't tell you why,' she replied indifferently. 'Ah, here is a cab. Goodbye, Poppy, and I might get you one of those little wooden apples for your birthday—'

But it was not a wooden apple that I wanted, still less a box. I longed for something else.

The very first pocket money day, my twenty copeks in a tiny purse, I ventured to go there again, my heart having been captured by a little polar bear—carved true in every detail. The shop was empty. The pleasant voice wished me good-morning. I answered the greeting shakily and cleared my throat. Would the little bear take the whole of my pocket money, I wondered secretly, and then asked the price.

'Fifty copeks,' replied the voice.

I gasped and murmured I was sorry.

'Why, *baryshna* (miss)?' asked the voice, and I explained. There followed a pause, and I moved nearer the door when the voice asked suddenly:

'Born here, were you?'

'Yes.'

'So was I. A good place to be born in. Teaches you a lot, the city does, for all some folk say to the contrary. When is your birthday, *baryshna*?'

Surprised, I told him the date.

'Will you then accept the little bear as a present?'

I blushed and stuttered as polite a refusal as I could think of. But the voice insisted and, presently, the treasure in my hand and the pocket money unspent, I hurried along Nicholas Quay. But never again did I enter that enchanted kingdom. Not having seen him, I knew he had seen me, and I felt that I just could not go there and not make a purchase.

Nor did I ever unravel the mystery. The exquisite things sold in that tiny place were certainly beyond the means of the poor folk, and customers with plenty of money to spend must have been as indifferent as my Aunt Catherine. Many a time did I pass the 'voice shop' since that day in the spring. Once, in the summer I saw two elegantly dressed little girls staring at the little table laden with the fruit and the animals. Their governess was evidently paying for what they had chosen, and I made to hurry on when I heard the shrill voice of one of the little girls:

'Why don't you ever come out? Have you got a lion's head, or what?'

The voice did not reply. Crimson with embarrassment, the governess hurried her charges out of the shop. Her voice thick with anger she started to scold, but I did not listen.

CHAPTER FIVE

Transport

FROM OLD engravings rather than from books did I learn early
enough that at the very beginning St Petersburg had no other
public transport than rowing boats and so called *odnokolkas*, a
cart on two wheels drawn by one horse. The *odnokolka* could
hardly have offered much comfort to its passengers: it had one
plank for a seat in the rear, another in front for the driver.
There was no hood, and the jolting of the iron wheels along
unpaved streets must have been ghastly. People of affluence
drove about in coaches, imported from Holland and Germany,
and crossed the river in their own luxuriously cushioned barges.
In winter, the *odnokolkas* had their iron wheels clamped on to

sled runners. When the ice over the Neva had thickened enough, the boatmen made a good livelihood by taking people across in stoutly-built wooden chairs set on iron runners, and that means of travelling had not changed down to my own days. The men were bred to the business, and they knew how to avoid what were known as 'black patches' where deceptively firm ice was really thin over quite a few square feet of unfrozen water.

The men, skates on their feet, ran like the wind, and to be taken in a chair across the Neva was one of the greatest pleasures —except that it did not last long, and there you were on the opposite bank, all of you glowing with the invigorating breaths of frost and wind.

In my childhood, public transport was varied and not uniformly cheap. Up and down Nevsky Prospect and along the more important streets ran the so called *konkas* (from *kon*, a horse), single-deck buses with two and sometimes four horses drawing them. They ran all through the four seasons, and were most uncomfortably cold in winter: there were no doors and no heating inside. In a sudden blizzard, and those happened often enough, you had to fight your way as best you could through a drift of snow to get in or out.

The first electric trams appeared in 1908, but people like us could seldom afford the fares. At the beginning those trams covered Nevsky Prospect from Nicholas Railway station down to Alexander Gardens. The start was not very fortunate—the current frequently breaking down. For my tenth birthday, i.e. in July 1908, my cousin Natalie made me a present of a double drive—up to Nicholas Station and back to Alexander Gardens where, she said, we would have chocolate and ices in the open air.

It fell on a gorgeous sunny day, and I looked forward to my 'present' immensely. We boarded the tram and it ran fast and smooth until it stopped with a terrific jerk half-way down the Prospect. '*Chtoto s tokom sluchiloss*' ('something has happened to the current'), said the conductor, adding with a grin: '*opiat*' ('again'). Natalie asked how long it would be before we started again and the man shrugged. After a few minutes, I leant out of the window: the bright red, orange and green trams seemed to stretch for miles on both lines. Natalie said: '

'We'd better get out and have our ices at *Aux Gourmets*. How lucky that it should be just opposite.'

Chocolate had been drunk; I had my two apricot and walnut ices. The trams were at a standstill. We came out to hear the loud laughter and mocking shouts from the drivers of horse carriages as they flashed past. We re-entered our tram. Within some few minutes we moved off at last only to stop again. All in all, it took nearly an hour to reach Znamensky Square and Nicholas Station. Natalie was annoyed, but I enjoyed it all.

By 1910, however, such incidents happened seldom, and many more tram-lines were laid down until they reached Vassily Island where we lived. It took people some time to get used to them. Trams ran at a speed wholly unfamiliar and therefore frightening; the accident rate rose alarmingly, and the police blamed the drivers and the passengers careless enough to get on and off while the tram was moving.

Horses and boats kept their pride of place in St Petersburg all through my childhood. With the exception of steamers plying up and down the Neva, mechanically propelled vehicles did not somehow answer the mood of the city. I can remember very few bicycles, and even the most wealthy people preferred their elegant carriages to automobiles. Up to 1917 there was but one taxi rank by the great colonnade of shops known as *Gostiny Dvor* (literally Merchants' Yard) down Nevsky Prospect. I had never ridden in one, and I heard it said that the chauffeurs charged exorbitant prices even for short journeys. Somehow, taxis were not considered 'respectable'. My Aunt Nadine, an officer's prim and sour-minded widow, who thought any woman 'fast' if she wore low-cut evening dresses and used scented soap, was once discussing a friend's daughter who had been staying with her.

'I could not very well refuse to have her but oh, her scented soap, her transparent petticoats, and her dreadful ideas about women being judges and professors! On top of it all, she hired one of those dreadful taxis to go to the station! I really don't know what our yard porter thought of it. Fortunately, it was raining and I did not see her off!'

'Yes, that rain was a piece of luck for you—' said my mother calmly.

For the ordinary people there were *droshky*, an oddly-shaped open carriage with iron wheels, straw on the floor and a hard flat leather cushion over the seat. It was drawn by a single horse with a hungry look and a tangled mane. The *vankas*, as the drivers were called, plied their trade all over the city. They drove slowly, lazily, and were quite peculiarly talkative. If their passengers did not share their passion for chatter, the *vankas* talked to their horses.

There was no set tariff, and nobody ever got into a *droshky* without prolonged chaffering. My cousin Boris, Natalie's gifted brother, who was an important person working with Golovin at décors for ballets and operas in the great studio at Mariinsky Theatre, once met me near Alexander Gardens.

'Like to be driven home?' he asked.

Speechless, I nodded, my face flushed with pleasure, and Boris hailed the nearest *droshky*.

'Vassily Island, 9th Line, No 44—'

The *vanka* sank into deep contemplation for a few seconds, then stroked his beard, looked at Boris and me, and mumbled:

'Quite a distance from here, sir, isn't it? Forty-five copeks, and I am not likely to gain by it either.'

'Thirty,' said Boris.

We moved on. So did the *droshky*.

'Forty, sir—'

'Thirty, I said.'

'Thirty-five, sir—'

Boris did not reply. Suddenly the man reined in, and we stopped too.

'All right, sir, but Christ be my witness—It's not enough to buy a bag of oats for him—'

Boris made no comment. We got in and moved off at the horse's pace which might have been compared to that of a snail. Yet what a pleasure it was to drive in a common *droshky*!

On some occasions, however, chaffering ended rather comically. My mother, who gave English lessons, had a wealthy Jewess among her pupils. The lady could be uncommonly generous and mean by turn. Once, the lesson ended and my mother having lent her some books, she said she had meant to bring some chocolates with her and would I go with her to her flat and fetch them.

We then lived in rooms in the 9th Line. The lady had a luxurious flat in Galernaya Street just across Nicholas Bridge. As soon as we came out, with me carrying the books, she said she felt tired and hailed a *droshky*. I forget the amount demanded by the *vanka*, but I remember her shrill, sharp voice:

'Twenty-five!'

On we walked, the *vanka* following. We crossed to the bridge, he still behind us. In less than ten minutes we reached Galernaya Street. *Vanka* sighed and raised his voice:

'All right! Have it your way, Madam.'

She did not answer. We were at the front door of her house.

Mounting the stairs to her first floor flat, she said triumphantly:
'Well, I do feel a bit tired, but I have saved twenty-five copeks!'

I still remember my relief when on coming out, with a big box of chocolates under my arm, I could not see that *vanka* in the street.

For more affluent people there were *likhachy*, a well-sprung carriage made all the more comfortable with soft rugs and velvet cushions, a beautifully groomed, well-fed horse, the harness all leather and silver, the driver sporting a coat of dark blue face cloth and a brown velvet cap trimmed with pheasant feathers. Nobody would dream of haggling with a *likhach*: you hailed him and gave the direction. He jumped off his box and arranged the rug neatly. Then, back on the box, he whistled, and the horse 'flew like lightning'. At the end, the fare was mentioned almost casually and, in accordance with custom, a fat tip, *na chay* was added. The *likhach*, cap in hand, bowed low from the hips, and wished 'good health to your Excellency'. Once only did I have such a drive with a friend and her mother. It was pleasant enough but secretly I knew I preferred the rough simplicity of a *droshky*, chiefly because of the *vankas*. They were all peasants, some from as far north as Archangel Province and some from the deep south, almost on the fringes of the Crimea. After a day's hard work, they were often too tired to give a good grooming to their horses, but I have heard of cases when a *vanka* would forego his own modest supper to provide a little more oats and hay for his nag. *Vankas* were a definitely Russian element in St Petersburg. Their garrulity was never boring. They spiced their talk with many ancient sayings such as 'flour will come out of corn' ('*peremeletzia—mouka budet*') and 'dear as an egg on Christ's day' ('*dorogo iachiyko ko Khristovou dniu*'), i.e., Easter. Their humour was dry and ironic. They had a peasant's philosophy and a peasant's faith. They never day-dreamt of making fortunes: they went to the capital to earn a livelihood and no more. Sometimes their fares cheated them, and a *vanka* had no means of redress. To the police, he was just one among thousands of so-called 'black people' (*cherniy liud*), and a complaint was so much wasted breath. They lived in appallingly squalid hostels in the slummiest parts of the city, and they never complained. Because of their raggedness, they were forbidden to drive along certain parts of the quays on the South Side, and they took it all in good part. Dear *vankas*, patient, wise and uncomplaining! Never sentimental about their horses, they cared for them deeply.

In the summer we had little blue steamers plying up and down the wide reaches of the Neva. The fares were cheap and we could use them often enough. We boarded at a jetty on Vassily Island and were carried off upstream, under one of the broadly-arched spans of Nicholas Bridge. The steamer would moor off the Admiralty Quay on the South Side, and then she crossed the river to the University Quay on the North Side, and went on to Viborg Side close to the Cathedral of SS. Peter and Paul. That brief halt behind, we went back to the South Side and stopped by the Summer Gardens where we usually got off. Then the little steamer plied on to the outlying islands, on the North Bank, the Little Ochta and the Great Ochta; and on beyond Alexander Bridge, sometimes even as far as Schlüsselburg at the mouth of the Neva, near to Ladoga Lake.

The return ticket from Vassily Island to the Summer Gardens was five copeks, a modest enough charge and well within our reach. Any such trip brought a sequence of discoveries. The steamer had a saloon deck, a restaurant and a bar, but I always preferred to be in the open. The islands on the North Side and on the South seemed incredibly different when seen from midstream. Even humble ochre-coloured buildings had a new glory bestowed on them.

And, on board, everything breathed pure magic. The blue-coated man at the wheel looked like someone dropped down from a different planet. The stewards in their tiny white jackets seemed like so many magicians capable of contriving an omelette out of a piece of leather. The throb of the engine rang like music, and the dark blue water when seen from the gunwale was like a phrase out of some fairy story. I would lean over to listen; the great Neva rippled and whispered: 'You belong to me,' and something within me whispered back: 'Yes, and you belong to me.'

No such poetic flashes came at railway stations, *vokzaly*, as they were called, but they offered enough excitement to draw me like a magnet. I remember four of them: the Tsarskoselsky, built in 1837, which joined the capital to its western suburbs, Tsarskoe Selo, Gatchina, Peterhof and others. That *vokzal* intrigued me vastly because on certain days the space in front of it would be cordoned off by black-coated police and no 'outsiders' were allowed to pass. On occasions, a closed carriage, drawn by two splendid bays, would drive up to the gates, and through a chink here and there it was possible to catch glimpses of elegant ladies accompanied by incredibly well-groomed men, and whispers would run about:

'The King of Portugal, is it?'

'No, no, the King of Italy!'

'Rubbish! It is the Grand-Duke of Hesse and his wife—'

'And here is the King of the Belgians, surely—'

There were tantalizing glimpses of ostrich feathers, diamonds, hands gloved in delicately coloured suède, and then all vanished, the Emperor's royal guests gone on the last lap of their journey to meet their host at Tsarskoe Selo. The police cordon melted away and the station looked as ordinary as the remains of a cold leg of mutton served for Monday's dinner.

At the end of Nevsky Prospect stood the enormous Nicholas

station, its trains bound for Moscow, Central Russia, and as far south as the Crimea and the Caucasus. On the north bank of the river stood the ugly ochre-coloured Finland *vokzal* from where people travelled to the northern suburbs of St Petersburg, and right through Finland to the Norwegian frontier. Ugly and forbidding as the building was, it always warmed my heart to see it because it was the gateway into Finland where my Danish grandmother lived in a low white house on an island in the middle of a lake.

But the most exciting of them all was Warsaw station from where fortunate people went abroad. The long train carried them as far as Verzhbolovo near the German frontier where they had to change because of the difference in railway gauges. So far as I can remember, there was no charge for platform tickets, but there were policemen mounting guard at the door of every coach, and a police inspector examined tickets and passports, and then whisked out a notebook to ask endless questions of every passenger. Where were they going? 'Name and address of the hotel', and so forth.

About once a year we went to Warsaw station to give a send-off to my mother's sister, my Aunt Fanny, who usually left for Rome where her elder sister lived. With an imperious air she would produce her ticket and passport. Then the inspector's notebook would appear.

'Name and address of the hotel, please?'

My Aunt Fanny's blue eyes flashed angrily.

'I am not going to any hotel, officer. I am going to my sister's.'

'Her name, please?'

'Countess Filippani-Ronconi—' and at the mention of a title, the inspector would snap his notebook, bow, and mumble:

'Please step into the coach, your Excellency, and I will see to your luggage.'

73

For no reason that I could tell that scene always made me giggle.

All in all I loved my excursions to the *vokzaly*. In my imagination, endless journeys were planned, begun and finished. It gave me great satisfaction to stand on a platform and watch the people about to board the trains, rich folk commanding the services of white-bloused porters and surrounded by masses of expensive luggage. There were other groups carrying their own belongings and having a determinedly genteel air. They were obviously second-class passengers. Finally, there were the third class folk, peasants, small traders and suchlike, with their straw baskets and clumsy bundles. The first and second class coaches had seats upholstered in red velvet and in rep. The third class cars had rough wooden benches and their occupants were not permitted to use the restaurant car. They had to carry their own provisions and tin kettles for hot water which they could get at any halt during the journey.

CHAPTER SIX

Neighbours and Others

ST PETERSBURG was the capital of Russia, and yet she had no true Russian 'feel' about her, *vankas* and a few others excepted. Great Italian and French architects designed her loveliest buildings. Her numerous cotton and paper mills, her shipyards and steel works had Englishmen, Germans and Dutchmen for their owners and managers. Her dressmakers, tailors, and glovers were mostly French, and her finest shoemakers—German or English. The best restaurants were French again—with the exception of *Medvied* ('the Bear'), though I heard it said that the Russian name screened an Italian proprietorship. The best private schools were German. St Petersburg had great orthodox cathedrals, but her population demanded their own places of worship: Lutheran, Anglican, Presbyterian, American Episcopalian and American Baptist, Dutch Calvinist, and a lovely St Louis des Français served by French Dominican Friars. The Poles again had their own cathedral as well as a big church, St Catherine's, on Nevsky Prospect. Many banks were in American, English, German and Dutch hands. There was not a single shop of importance but displayed boldly lettered notices: 'English spoken', '*Ici on parle Français*' and '*Man spricht Deutsch*', and it was difficult for any man or women to find employment in such shops unless they knew at least two foreign languages.

Along the busy waterfront, right up to Nicholas Bridge, it meant no effort to travel far and wide—imaginatively. Here stood a portly Dutch skipper talking slow, broken English to an American. A few yards away, leaning against the rail of a gangway, a wiry, swarthy Spaniard might be arguing about his cargo with a tall, blond Norwegian. The Spaniard spoke a terribly broken French. The Scandinavian's German sounded more convincing but, looking at them, I knew that neither understood the other. I walked on and saw a burly bearded Russian stevedore bending to examine a damaged crate and showering curses on two or three Italian sailors who, frowning at the crate, kept shaking their heads, and it was obvious that the Russian oaths were wholly beyond their understanding.

Even a brief walk along that waterfront was worth more than a dozen geography lessons. There breathed a mingled fragrance of unfamiliar spices, oranges, lemons, vanilla and tar. There was the sense of remote open seas all over the wide river, and it was good to remember that even the tiniest stream threaded its stubborn way towards one of the Neva's four tributaries and thus eventually ran into the Gulf of Finland. The world seemed at once small and immense.

At many corners up and down Nevsky Prospect I saw tall

dark Circassians, their sheepskin capes, worn even on the hottest summer day, fastened with tarnished silver buckles. They crouched over gaily coloured rugs spread on the pavement and shouted their wares in deep throaty voices. They sold Circassian jewellery—mostly bangles and brooches of silver studded with turquoise, and their national sweets, in particular, candied walnuts. Some of those pedlars set up odd-looking iron braziers and baked *lavasky*, wafer-thin round cakes. The police did not trouble themselves about the Circassians, but one had to be cautious when dealing with them. They pretended not to understand Russian and were apt to argue about change. They belonged to the summer of St Petersburg: sharply-bladed autumn winds sent them flying back to their native mountains in the deep South.

There was yet another stratum of population firmly settled in St Petersburg, the Tartars who came from Kazan, the Crimea and other parts of the Empire. They were divided into three social grades. At the top were the Imperial household servants whose duty was to sweep all the palace courtyards and the quay. They wore cinnamon-coloured coats of rough cloth reaching below the knees and odd little caps trimmed with silver braid. There were many of them sweeping up and down Palace Quay, their yellow faces impassive and their spatulate fingers clutching the brooms as though they were so many swords. I looked at them with respect, but I never spoke to any of them. They were part of St Petersburg and yet they seemed unpleasantly alien.

The second grade consisted of restaurant waiters. They wore short white coats and aprons, and their yellow faces seemed all the darker because of their uniform. They were very clean, civil, and most efficient, and I heard that they were held in great respect by their managers—chiefly because of their honesty and sobriety. My cousin Alexander gave a dinner party

to some of his fellow officers at *Donon*, one of the most exclusive restaurants. The serving having been superlatively good, he called the maître d'hôtel to settle the bill and added a magnum of champagne to the lavish tip. The Tartar's face remained as impassive as ever, and he spoke very politely:

'I thank your Excellency, but we are all strict Muslims.'

'Well?'

'And we never touch wine.'

My cousin had forgotten what everybody, including himself, knew very well. He then tried to turn his slip into a joke!

'Not even in this place?'

'Most particularly not in this place,' replied the Tartar. He murmured his thanks for the tip and told the wine-waiter to take the champagne back to the cellar.

The lowest grade of all were the so-called *Khalaty*, and they terrified me. They were not allowed to ply their trade in the better parts of the city but Vassily Island teemed with them. They looked for cast-off clothes and other junk. Most of them were very tall. All of them were dirty and unkempt; summer and winter they wore a patched-up and stained *khalat*, half coat, half dressing-gown, reaching down to their ankles, with an equally dirty striped sack flung over the left shoulder. They would enter any yard, raise their heads, and shout '*Khalat! Khalat!*' If a face appeared at a window and a hand beckoned them, they would run to the door, mount the back stairs, find the right entrance, and plunge into an endless chaffering in the kitchen of the flat. They spoke broken Russian, but could be extremely eloquent. What cooks we had usually came from the Baltic Provinces and were very clean and tidy women. They hated a *khalat* in their kitchen—but they could not very well say so when my mother wanted to get rid of an old coat or a worn-out skirt.

I did not hate them: I was terrified of them. If, on returning from a wander, I heard their piercing shout in the yard, I would keep away until I saw the *khalat* come out and walk off in the opposite direction. Their height, their dark yellow faces deeply grooved with dirt, and, in particular, their green-and-blue-striped sacks, all scared me. I imagined that nothing could have prevented them from picking me up and shoving me inside one of those awful sacks. Yet frightened as I was, I could never keep away from the kitchen once a *khalat* was there. I suppose my mother's presence and the cook's lent me courage.

Once summoned, the *khalat* would take off his extremely dirty cap, bow, and kneel by the window to examine whatever my mother had to sell. Then still kneeling, he would raise his head and say with a sigh:

'Poor stuff, lady, very old.'

'I would not be selling it if it were new,' answered my mother.

'Very poor stuff,' sighed the *khalat*, 'but my sack is empty, lady. Forty copeks for both.'

My mother shook her head.

'Seventy-five for the coat and twenty-five for the skirt.'

'Robbing a poor Tartar, lady—'

'Let him go, Madam,' murmured the cook.

But the haggling went on until the *khalat* sighed again.

'Sixty copeks—lady—my sack empty! Sixty copeks,' he pleaded, rising from his knees.

'Eighty,' replied my mother, adding, 'and that is my last word.'

'Ah well,' he mumbled, 'my sack—empty, and now my purse empty too.'

The coins were put on a window-sill. I knew that the cook would presently wash them in hot soapy water. They certainly looked dirty. The garments vanished into the sack, and still the *khalat* stayed on.

'Anything else, lady? See my sack not full—'

'No.'

'A carpet now, or a blanket—some china? Me buy everything —me pay well.'

'Nothing at all. Please go.'

He went, sighing deeply. If it were winter, the cook would burn a sprig or two of mint in the kitchen. In the summer she would fling the window wide open to get rid of the smell left by the *khalat* and his striped sack.

It was my imaginative reading of history that created the terror. The palace servants and waiters were clean, led a disciplined life, and were decently clothed. But the *khalaty*, their kinsmen by blood, were a tribe apart. Their height, their incredible dirt and throaty 'nagging' voices, all alike appalled me, and involuntarily I thought about all the horrors of the Tartar invasion of Russia in the thirteenth century. Their savage hordes pillaged and ravaged the country from East to West, from North to South, and then settled down on the conquered land. 'The Tartar Yoke', as it came to be known, lasted for nearly two centuries.

It was an ancient enough story, but its remoteness drew nearer and nearer until it merged with the present in my unruly imagination. I felt that I would not be surprised to see a *khalat*, having haggled his fill over a frayed curtain, draw a short curved sword out of his sack and cut off the cook's head then and there.

It was a most unreasonable terror. The *khalaty* were by far the most law-abiding people in St Petersburg. They paid their taxes, they gave no trouble, they never got drunk or encroached upon the streets to them forbidden. For all their passion for haggling, they never stooped to cheating: you did not have to count the change they gave. Briefly, they were the rather convenient dustbins of St Petersburg.

★

There were crowds of unremarked, unchronicled and hard-working men and women, who plodded their way through heat-waves and iron frosts, found it difficult to make ends meet and never complained, and were, however inarticulately, aware of the beauty surrounding them. St Petersburg was theirs in a very particular way.

There was Akulina once apprenticed to a court dressmaker and accustomed to handle fine silks, lace and velvet. Her apprenticeship about to end, Akulina was stricken with a disease which made her hands clumsy and sometimes useless and her legs swollen up to the knee. The French dressmaker was not quite stony of heart: she sent the girl to the Obukhovsky Hospital where she was declared to be incurable. So Akulina counted her meagre savings and moved from the silken, scented splendour of a house on Fontanka Quay to a small bed-sitter on the third floor of a tenement in one of the cheapest streets on Petersburg Side. There, forgetting all about court gowns, Akulina took to earning her livelihood by darning, mending, and sometimes hemming sheets and pillow cases when her hands 'behaved'. I knew her well. The single window of her room gave her a generous view of the Neva, and she would chuckle:

'Ah, Miss, this is better than that narrow Fontanka Canal, God be praised for His mercies.'

When my mother and I lived in rooms on the 9th Line of Vassily Island, we found a small oil-shop close by. Its owner, an elderly hunchback bachelor, was Hans Andersen and Grimm rolled into one. I used to go there for candles and matches. The things paid for, I lingered and, if there were no other customers and that happened often enough, the little man always broke into a fairy story.

'Now there is a fir on the bank of the Zhdanovka River, a very old fir to look at, but it had not always been a tree. It had begun life as a king, and he lived on that island in a green-and-white palace and he ate his dinner off silver. Once, as he sat at table, his godmother came in, and she was a tiny, tiny fairy, and she wore a little bonnet made of white lilac petals. The king lifted her on to the table, and she leant against a gold salt cellar and told him never to marry a girl with green eyes. The king laughed because no such girls lived on his island and he never travelled beyond it. The fairy godmother shook her tiny head, and asked to be put down on the floor, and went away. A few days later the king met a girl with large, grey eyes, and he wished to make her his queen—so beautiful she was. They had a grand wedding, but the fairy godmother would not come.

'Well, after a while, the queen said she wished for a bonnet made of white lilac petals, and the king said no, white lilac petals were only used by fairies. The queen got angry, and the king saw that her large grey eyes were changing colour: at first, they darkened, then the greyness vanished, and she stood there, cheeks flushed, hands clenched, and her large eyes—green. "I want such a bonnet, and I shall have it!" she screamed. The king left the room and sent for one of his ministers. Every white lilac bush on the island was to be uprooted and planted elsewhere, and the queen was not to be told. Yet, being a witch, she heard of it and such was her rage that then and there she had her husband turned into a fir, and his godmother could not help him because he had disregarded her warning.'

'You have seen that old fir?' I ventured, and he replied soberly:

'Yes, but from a distance. Nobody is foolish enough to get near it.'

Then there was the 'Baltic Baroness', who part-owned No 44 together with many of her kin. Her own part could not have been very large, but she behaved as though she owned millions.

She lived in one room on the ground floor of that immense building, and her exalted relations never came to see her, but she strutted about as though she were queen of the Baltic, her small blue eyes missing nothing. She was short and fat, and she wore a startling yellow wig and three large cameo brooches on her vast bosom. In the summer she appeared in lilac print dresses. In the winter she wore purple. Presumably she was a widow, but nobody knew for certain. I remember her chiefly because of an odd sociological argument.

Two or three times a week we had a welcome visitor, a neat bent-shouldered Esthonian farmer's wife, who had her steading by the sea not far from Peterhof. She had a blind husband, her son was a fisherman, and she managed the little farm on her own. She brought fish, eggs, butter and cheese. As neat as a new pin she was, and merely to see her was to remember an April sunrise. I came to love her dearly, and I always followed her down the stairs, across the yard and shook hands with her at the gates.

One morning, having just seen her off, I turned and there stood the 'Baltic Baroness', her blue eyes blazing. She hissed at me:

'You are a nobleman's daughter and that woman is a peasant.'

I merely stared.

'And I saw you shake hands with her—'

That was an easy one to answer.

'Anyone would shake hands with a friend, wouldn't they? And she is a very dear friend.' I added, 'She smells of the sea—'

'I wouldn't care if she smelt of spices,' retorted the Baroness. 'She is a peasant and should keep her distance.'

'She is a friend,' I repeated stubbornly, and she flung at me:

'I shall complain to your mother. I can't have my tenants behave familiarly with such scum!'

'But I don't know any scum, Baroness,' I flung back and ran away.

One bleak autumn day she died, and I don't remember who stepped into her shoes at No 44, but I do remember that I felt unashamedly glad to hear of her going: she did not belong to St Petersburg. Indeed, she belonged nowhere.

There was a stationer's shop not far from the Naval College on Nicholas Quay. It was kept by a very kindly man and his extremely cross wife. He would tell me he could not live anywhere except in St Petersburg. She grumbled that the fogs and the floods were enough to drive you crazy, but both were born and bred there and would never have settled down anywhere else. I would go in to buy a little paper or a few pencils. He smiled. She scowled.

'A lovely sunset last night—' he said, wrapping up my humble purchases.

'A terrible wind this morning,' she retorted.

'They say we're going to have a mild winter—' he went on and she interrupted:

'Yes, so they say! Just you wait and see! Blizzards and blizzards—'

'Well, what about leaving?'

'Leaving? Are you mad? Where else should we go?' and I knew that she loved St Petersburg as much as I did. And that was the spell the city wove round about you. It was a tapestry of delicate beauty and much squalor, but somehow the former gained over the latter.

There were the police—the rank and file in black, sergeants and inspectors in grey-blue. I was far too young at the time to understand why the majority of people disliked and mistrusted them. I knew nothing about the bribes they took or about the harsh treatment they meted out to 'the suspects' and those under arrest. In all my wanderings about the city only once did I see a policeman strike a woman, and it greatly shocked me because of its singularity. Otherwise I knew them as upholders of order, sometimes stiff and abrupt in their manner, but invariably helpful and even heroic in the spells of disaster such as a flood or a fire.

I remember a spring day in 1909; the morning lessons over, I went for a long wander which ended at the gateway of the Summer Gardens. The day had seemed mild and calm, but a sudden gust of wind all but swept me off my feet, and I turned back. There were two large open spaces to cross before I reached Nicholas Bridge—Mars Meadow and Senate Square. By the time I reached the bridge, a fierce gale was raging and my heart all but failed me. The middle of the bridge was certainly safe, but it carried double tram-lines and the usual to-and-fro of horse traffic. I had not a copper to hire a *droshky*. I stood at the quay corner, buffeted by the fierce gusts, irresolute and very near tears, when a tall burly policeman came up to me:

'Crossing the bridge, *baryshna*, are you?'

I nodded, too miserable to remember I had a voice to use.

'Come on then—'

He gripped my left elbow and piloted me right into the middle of the bridge. There were trams, lorries, *droshkys*, private carriages to the right and to the left, but the man steered his way unerringly, guided me across the perilous slope of Nicholas Square at the end of the bridge, and would not let me go until I had assured him that my home was quite near.

'Ah, the wind can be cruel,' he said, brushed away my thanks with a shrug and turned back to the perils of the bridge.

*

Rank on rank, the sons and daughters of St Petersburg rise in the memory: the shabby university students, some among whom would have starved unless they gave 'outside' lessons in their few hours of leisure; the uncomplaining crowd of minor civil servants, whose usual diet consisted of weak tea, thinly buttered bread and herrings, and whose wives could afford a new hat about once in five years and were sometimes hard put to it to settle a cobbler's modest bill; glossy, self-satisfied shop-keepers; sturdy apple-women, a tattered shawl all too often their only protection through the winter months; casual pedlars and crippled beggars with their stubborn faith in charity . . . boys and young men from state schools and colleges, all wearing their appointed uniforms—black, blue, or grey with multi-coloured facings. Infantry officers and men and guardsmen resplendent in crimson, blue and white, their knee-high boots polished like so many mirrors. Plump, well-dressed doctors and lawyers so obviously proud of the plush-covered chairs in their waiting-rooms; and streaks of poverty again and again seen on the bearded face of a *vanka* and in the rags of a stevedore and so many others since real poverty occupied much of the landscape and did not slink into dark corners.

Finally, there were the grand people from the South Side, who drove in splendid carriages and went home to mansions where high, painted ceilings were supported by pillars of green marble and porphyry, where no footsteps were ever heard be-cause of the thick carpets, where meals were served by men-servants in plush breeches. . . . In three or four of those mansions lived distant cousins on my mother's side, and on very rare occasions we were invited to a meal with them. They were all rich but not really hard-hearted about our own poverty: it just did not exist for them, or else, what was much more likely, the mere idea of easing it would have appalled them since, as I think now, they considered we had no business to be poor because of the crest on our very modest quantity of silver. To the real, low-born poor those people were generous enough.

Far too much has been written and said about their domestic luxuries; far too little about all the generous gestures in founding and upkeeping of hospitals, maternity homes, schools in the country and many more. . . .

On them all, rich and poor alike, the city stamped her peculiar impress, compelled them to enjoy her beauty and to endure the vagaries of her climate.

Nicholas Bridge

CHAPTER SEVEN

Blue Waterways and Green Pleasances

THE NEVA has four main tributaries which, in their turn, receive the waters of innumerable little rivers and streams. All of them together, with a sea to the west and an enormous lake to the east, justified St Petersburg being called the Venice of the North. Yet that multitude of waters could not have satisfied either Peter the Great or his immediate successors, because they had canals dug here, there and everywhere. Few were the streets without one bridge or even more along their length. All in all there were a hundred and fifty bridges, some of them known to me by name only.

Four were built across the Neva: Nicholas Bridge with exquisite bronze griffons on its railings, Palace Bridge which joined the eastern tip of Vassily Island to the South Side, Trinity Bridge linking the vast Mars Meadow to the fashionable Kammenostrovsky Avenue on the North Bank and, finally, Alexander Bridge in the neighbourhood of Finland Station.

They were all majestic and very beautiful, but I preferred the little bridges spanning lesser rivers, canals and streams, Exchange, Chain, Police, Red, Blue, Catherine, Laundry (*Pracheshny Most*)—so called because in the old days washer-women of the city had the right to do their work there. Probably the loveliest of all was the Lions' footbridge across one of the canals, with four bronze animals, two at each end, guarding its delicate spans.

The Neva was the queen among rivers to me. Otherwise, the most cherished reach of running water was the Swan Stream (*Lebiazhia Kanavka*) flowing between the north side of the Summer Gardens and Mars Meadow. A beautiful footbridge spanned it. The stream did not belie its name: swans did glide up and down its clear dark waters. The biographer of Anna Pavlova mentioned that it was precisely there, while watching together with Michael Fokin two lordly swans vanish downstream towards the massive Sappers' Castle, that the great ballerina, then still in her teens, first had the idea of her *Dying Swan*.

That spot was lovely through all the seasons, but particularly in the late spring. The garden there had been thickly planted with lilac, heliotrope, pink and white. Opposite the footbridge the lilacs, as it were, stepped back, forming a perfect semi-circle, with a plain grey granite bowl, set on a high pedestal, in the middle, and a small granite bench close to the bridge. The wind from the Neva was sometimes unkind to the lilacs, but the little stream gained in beauty from the delicately coloured petals falling on its breast.

So quiet and nearly always deserted was the place that often in spring and summer I would tramp there, a satchel crammed with lesson books, a few sandwiches and an apple or two, slung over my shoulder.

The food would be eaten, but alas for the lesson books! Dutifully pulled out of the satchel, they lay undisturbed on the warm silken grass. How could anyone think of the Himalayas, French and German verbs or geometry when at any moment, as I knew well, some three or four swans, accompanied by their mates, might appear and glide past noiselessly and yet musically. I was rarely robbed of my hope, and I felt that, even when gone from sight, they left something of their proud beauty on the water.

It was just there that I came to experience a sharp humiliation.

It must have been some feast day or other in late spring (in 1911, I think) because I had no lessons that morning. When I got near the Swan Stream and began crossing the footbridge, I saw that the small bench was occupied by a rather untidy girl in her early twenties. She wore no hat and her unkempt blonde hair kept falling over her face. I saw that her grey canvas shoes were even shabbier than mine. She had a thick book in her lap and two or three more lay on the bench beside her. I guessed her as belonging to the first women's college in St Petersburg. She took no notice of me and went on brushing the hair off her forehead.

Now I always preferred grass to any bench and I knew perfectly well that the Summer Gardens were public, but quite unreasonably I resented that girl's presence. I passed by the bench and sprawled on the grass, the unopened satchel at my feet. Within a few minutes the place was further invaded by a slim man in his early thirties. He came through the gap in the lilacs, passed me, and went towards the bridge. Then he turned back and I saw what remarkable *live* eyes he had. He took no notice of the girl on the bench but she, her hair swept off her face, simply stared and stared at him.

'I believe we have met before,' he said to me.

I scrambled to my feet. I had a feeling that I had met him before, but I could not remember where or when, and in my clumsiness I said so.

'At your Aunt Catherine's—' He smiled. 'My name is Blok.'

It said nothing at all to me though I had enough sense not to tell him so, and mumbled that I thought my mother was taking me there one day the following week.

'I know. They have invited me, too, so we'll meet again—' He lifted his hat, bowed, went back to the bridge and vanished across Mars Meadow.

No sooner had he gone than the girl student flung her book aside and rushed towards me.

'You know *him*!' she cried shrilly.

I was so taken aback that it was a minute before I could reply. Yes, I had met the gentleman at the house of one of my relations and it seemed that I was going to meet him again.

'But I don't really know him—'

She stared at me with boundless contempt.

'To have met *him* and not to know who *he* is!'—she kept stressing the pronoun savagely. 'Talk of pearls before swine! I'd have given everything just to tell him that I live on his poetry—but I did not dare, I did not dare.'

Then I remembered. It was Alexander Blok, regarded by so

many people as the greatest poet since the days of Pushkin and Lermontov. I should never have forgotten having met him, and I certainly did not deserve the still greater honour of being recognized by him. Deeply incensed as I was by the girl's rudeness, I felt even more deeply humiliated by my own clumsy manner towards the poet.

'And who is that relation of yours where you are going to meet him again?' she flung at me so savagely that for all answer I stooped, picked up the satchel and made for the gap between the lilacs. The repeated insult 'pearls before swine' reached me clearly enough, and I knew it was not altogether undeserved.

An hour or so later I ventured to get back to the little sanctuary. The stone bench was empty, there was nobody in sight, and to my great relief I was never to meet the girl again.

*

There was a little wooden bridge spanning the none-too-wide Zhdanovka River well to the east of Petersburg Side. Its iron railings were not high and it could not have been of any importance: it bore the name of 'Poustoy'—i.e. 'Empty'. I can't remember if it was open to horse traffic. The banks of the Zhdanovka were girdled with thick-girthed limes. Behind stood tiny one-storied stone houses and still smaller wooden huts, and the winding street was left unpaved. Fishermen, small shopkeepers, pedlars and apprentices lived there and, presumably, worshipped in an ugly church with a slanting wooden porch and a crazy little belfry. But the humble little bridge has stayed vividly in the memory.

I can't remember what exactly brought me to discover it because apart from the generous shade of the trees, the environment offered no excitements and the waters of the Zhadnovka ran clear only after a good long rainfall. It was certainly raining the morning I reached it; and the wooden planks of the Poustoy were treacherously slippery so that the iron railing was good to hold on to. Just in front of me, a great basket of apples on her left arm, trotted a tiny plump lady in a black sateen skirt and a sky-blue shawl. She had already crossed when she slipped, the basket tilting forward, and in a moment the muddy ground glittered with golden and red apples. Fortunately, the ground sloping down from the river, the fruit did not roll into the water, but I heard the little woman's cry of distress, hurried towards her, and measured my length on the very last lap. Her own trouble forgotten, she turned and ran towards me.

I picked myself up. Together we gathered up the apples, their colours sadly in abeyance because of the mud. We found a bench somewhere, and she pulled out a huge blue handkerchief and started cleaning the fruit. When the handkerchief got too muddy, I ran with it to the lip of the little river and got it clean again. When the very last apple had been rubbed to perfection, she leant back and laughed. Not a word had we yet said to each other, and when she spoke, her very broken Russian told me that she was Finnish.

'You are a very kind young lady. See, the rain has stopped. Take off your coat—it is so wet—but the wet won't hurt the apples. Please, how many could you carry in your little coat? Ten? Fifteen?'

'One—' I told her.

She was like an apple herself—round, rosy-cheeked, glossy and clean.

'Ah—but you don't look a rich young lady to me. You could do with ten—' she insisted, and I felt that the bridge should have been called '*dobry*'—i.e. 'good' or 'kindly'.

In the end I had half a dozen apples and carried them home very carefully.

She had never asked me for my name, nor had I ventured to put a single question to her, but both of us had guessed that we belonged to every reach of running water in St Petersburg. We were never to meet again.

*

Indeed, in broad terms, the city was all water and green pleasances. All the Lines on Vassily Island had trees along their pavements, and there was a separate green kingdom on the University Quay—Roumiantzev Garden, which had a rather heavy bronze monument to the great field-marshal in its heart, but there were also many excitingly curved paths bordered by old elms and limes. I heard it said by someone that the garden had once formed part of the huge park of Menshikov Palace, the first stone mansion to be built in the city soon after its foundation in 1703. Certainly, its trees looked old enough.

The streets of most of the nineteen islands were fringed with trees even those on Petersburg Side which had no other large green pleasance than the church gardens neighbouring a belfry reputed to be haunted. We spent one summer there and I never lost my heart to the gardens. They looked dusty; they were always crowded, and there was not a single corner to cherish in the memory.

On the South Side both Alexander and Summer Gardens were beautiful. The former had a long alley bordered with tall silver birches, their satin bark glorious in the sunlight and very comforting on dull grey days. A swing was hung between two of the trees and, whilst rocking to and fro on the narrow wooden seat, I often built pictures in my mind. I knew that sooner or later I would have to go to school, and then on to university, there to read History; and later, of course, there would be my living to earn since we were very poor. But those were facts, and I did not waste time on facts among the silver birches in Alexander Gardens. I imagined myself spending my entire life in St Petersburg, delving more and more deeply into her endlessly varied magic. I saw myself building a small wooden house close to the Swan Stream, watching the swans through the summer months and studying hard through the long, long winter, daylight lasting sometimes less than five hours out of the twenty-four. I was neither young nor old in those fantasies: there seemed no time at all.

That very dear pleasance, Alexander Gardens, was nearly ruined for me in the summer of 1907 when I first met the woman in brown. She was small and elderly, but she was running down an avenue with the speed of a young girl. Under a shabby straw hat her face was brown and very wrinkled and her eyes glinted in a most peculiar way. I felt that she did not, as it were, belong anywhere, and her clothes suggested a poverty far sharper than mine. I felt sorry for her. Then she passed me, gave me a strange look, and muttered: 'I must poison the potatoes. I must poison the potatoes. You have heard me, haven't you?' and she stopped and stared at me.

There were uniformed keepers: there were other children playing, their nurses and governesses seated on the benches, but I felt very much alone and rather frightened. Who were those poisoned potatoes for? I seized the hoop and made for my favourite avenue. It looked quite deserted. I was running along when I heard steps gaining on me. I turned, and there she was. I almost dropped the hoop and plunged into a little path to the left. She followed me. I could still hear her muttering when, panting and dishevelled, I came within sight of the gates. There stood the keeper. I felt like bursting into tears, but my eyes were dry.

The woman in brown stopped, and the keeper moved towards her.

'Now, lady, you know you should not come here by your-self. Given the slip to the nurse again, haven't you?'

'I must poison the potatoes—' she told him when from a side path there appeared a middle-aged nurse and took the old woman away. The keeper sighed.

'Poor soul! But she would not hurt a fly, *baryshna*. Ah, the drab rags she wears! Nobody would think she lives in a grand flat in Gogol Street with carpets, palms, velvet curtains and all. I know—once I took her back there. That nurse has no wit at all. But the poor old soul would not hurt a fly,' he repeated.

'Why the poisoned potatoes?' I asked.

'Her Maker might know. I don't.'

Yet for all his persuasion, it was a long time before I went to Alexander Gardens again. There was an oddity and a mystery woven together. That poor woman was wealthy for all her shabbiness; she could afford a nurse, very likely had a carriage, and lived in one of the most exclusive parts of St Petersburg.

Well away from the great waterfront, in a grim grey street, stood a tall building, all its windows barred and its gates closed. It was St Nicholas' Hospital where the poorest of the poor were housed at the Government's expense. St Petersburg had its dark corners and I always thought St Nicholas' Hospital was the darkest of them all. It had the air of a prison rather than a hospital. It was huge, and I wondered how such a lovely city could have bred so many mad people. A maid of ours had a brother there, and she visited him when he was well enough to see her. From her I learned that there was a big garden at the back, that their food was plentiful, that the nurses were not uniformly kind, that they had a beautiful chapel and a benevolent old priest for chaplain.

'There are doctors too,' said the girl, 'but they might just as well not be there. The poor folk are seldom ill, and nothing is done to cure them of madness. Once they are in, they stay.'

Twice only did I pass that grim unhappy house and tried not to think too much of its inmates.

*

The Summer Gardens were spacious, beautiful and aristocratic. English, French and German governesses and nurses with expensive prams sat firmly on lime-wood benches keeping an eye on their elegantly dressed charges, and gossiping in three languages—usually about the iniquities of their employers, and the unspeakable climate of the city. Their charges kept strictly to their own set, and my usual shabbiness, to say nothing of my shyness, kept me away from them. But they all vanished in late spring either to the country or abroad, and were not seen till the winter. They belonged to the Mayfair of St Petersburg, the quays and the streets of the South Side, a world of carriages, liveried footmen, palms-on-staircases, velvet curtains and Persian carpets. Yet, however reluctantly, I had to admit that the Summer Gardens were theirs as much as mine, that they were children of the city as much as I was, and it seemed stupid to envy their elegantly cut coats of beige and pigeon's-egg blue and their kid gloves worn even at play. They were in charge of their governesses and nurses and they had not the liberty I enjoyed to explore any corner at my pleasure.

There were a great many other pleasances, and one of the greatest annual treats was a day spent on the Apothecaries Island with its exquisite botanical gardens. I can't now remember if you had to pay for going in—but I can still see row upon row of low-roofed glasshouses sheltering rare plants from all the corners of the globe, and the small walled-in herb garden started by the first doctors to settle in St Petersburg. In a little hut close by you could buy small silk and paper bags of dried herbs, with a label carrying instructions in Russian, French and Latin.

Behind the herb garden you came to a short avenue planted with bear-berry bushes; I believe their colour was red-orange, but I cannot tell if they were good for eating. The bushes gave way to old limes and, at the end, surrounded by tall trees, stood a grey stone house with a gracefully colonnaded porch. Its back windows gave you a view of the Neva gleaming dark-blue between the moss-embroidered tree trunks. There, they served tea, hot milk, and rather oddly-coloured herbal drinks. For food you could have potatoes baked in their skins, star-shaped meat patties and honey cakes, round, plump and fragrant. My mind full of herbal lore, I drank the milk and ate the golden-crusted patties, and the Apothecaries Island bade fair to outrival my affection for the Swan Canal.

Yet it lay so far from my home and could never be more than an annual treat. . . . All the same, it seemed both easy and pleasurable to turn that day into another star in my childhood's sky.

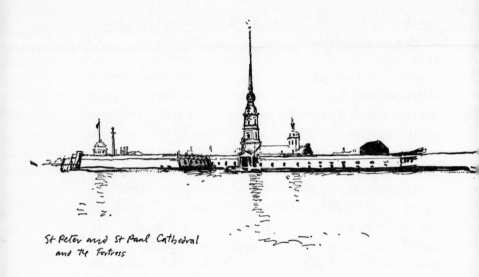

St Peter and St Paul Cathedral
and the Fortress

CHAPTER EIGHT

Palaces, Slums and Places of Enlightenment

THERE were quite a number of splendid private houses on the South Bank with big plate-glass windows and statues edging the roof, but their splendour never raised them to the level of palaces. *Dvoretz* (palace), meant a home of one or other member of the Imperial family, and in my early days that family suggested a clan, so many they were. The Emperor Nicholas I (1825–1855) had several sons, all of whom were married and acquired large families of their own. Nicholas's successor, Alexander II (1855–1881), had six sons.

Most of these palaces stood along the South waterfront, and in my wanderings along the quays, I often met one or other of the Grand-Dukes, all of them in military or naval uniforms since all were either soldiers or sailors, and no officer ever appeared in civilian clothes. They strode along, sometimes accompanied by a dog, but no equerry, still less a detective followed them. It was easy enough to recognize a Romanov— so tall they were and so graceful their carriage. Along the quay I often met Grand-Duke Peter and Grand-Duke Nicholas. In the Summer Gardens I sometimes came face to face with the poet, Grand-Duke Constantine, occasionally accompanied by his sister, Queen Olga of the Hellenes. Policemen and soldiers would salute them. Civilians did not.

It was in 1907 when I was about nine, that, always interested in markets, I made my way to Sennaya Place, by far the biggest market in the city. It stood well back off Sadovaya Street and unless my memory betrays me it lay at quite a distance from Nevsky Prospect; I know that I had not expected it to be either so big or so crowded. The deafening shouts of the stallholders and the no-less loud voices of the shoppers plunged me into confusion. Somehow or other I worked my way across the square and found myself in a tangle of narrow unfamiliar streets which ran in all directions. I knew I was lost and there did not seem to be a single policeman in sight to help me find my way to some well known haunt. I turned right and left until I reached a very quiet little square, a small bronze monument and a fountain in the middle. I stood on the edge of the pavement and a very elegant open carriage, drawn by a beautiful bay, went slowly by, its only occupant a middle-aged officer.

The sense of lostness must have been reflected on my face. The officer tapped the coachman's shoulder and he reined in at once. The officer leapt out, came across and asked me what the matter was.

'I have lost my way,' I stammered.

'Where do you live?'

I told him. He walked back to the carriage, gave an order to the coachman and vanished round the corner. Within a few seconds, the carriage drew level with the pavement.

'Jump in, young lady,' said the coachman rather gruffly, 'I have my orders to drive you to Vassily Island and, Lord God, isn't it a distance!'

I felt at once happy and confused. I never saw the small gilt crown on the carriage door or the row of medals on the coachman's breast. I luxuriated in the crimson velvet upholstery and the wonder of it all. The coachman did not talk.

When we reached the house on the 9th Line of Vassily Island, the burly yard porter on duty stared, rubbed his eyes and sprang to attention. Then he saw me and grinned from ear to ear.

'Yes—' grumbled the coachman, 'and now I have to trek all the long way back. But that is his Imperial Highness all over. Hardly a day do I take him for a drive but we must meet with a child or an animal in trouble. Last time we brought a lost kitten back to the palace and wasn't it filthy!'

The tall officer was Grand-Duke Dimitry, the poet's brother. Had I not been so shy, I might have told the coachman that my first cousin, Alexander, was one of Grand-Duke Constantine's equerries.

Foremost among all the Imperial mansions was the Winter Palace, a huge building, its face to the Neva and its back to the immense Palace Square. But the Emperor and his family gave up living there since the Russo-Japanese war in 1904, when they moved to Tsarskoe Selo, and the great palace always looked sad to me. It seemed too big and stonily-cold ever to be anyone's home. Once only did I get inside—in June 1914 when Admiral Beatty's squadron came to St Petersburg, and I conducted a party of petty officers and ratings from H.M.S. *Princess Royal* on a sight-seeing tour. I had been given a permit for the Winter Palace, and we were led through the state apartments and the chapel. The state rooms were just a series of immense, chilly halls, Nicholas, St George's, the Concert and the Malachite Halls. I believe there were a few others, but I can't remember their names. A scarlet-liveried guide kept talking about the furniture, the pictures and statues and about the splendour of great occasions in the past, but I was not listening to him. A window drew me and I gasped at the delight of the view— with the queenly river running below, and away to the left cupolas and spires of the SS. Peter and Paul Cathedral, a mausoleum rather than a church where all the Romanovs since Peter the Great, with the exception of his grandson Peter II, buried in Moscow, lay under their white marble sarcophagi.

It was a perfect day to match a perfect view. The distances were veiled in pale blue pearly haze. All the buildings on the North Bank seemed washed in gold that had streaks of silver in it. Even the grim Fortress wore a festival air.

Further along the same Palace Quay stood the home of Grand-Duke Wladimir with its famous raspberry-coloured drawing-rooms. Down by the corner of Mars Meadow was a palace almost as big as the Emperor's; it housed the poet, Grand-Duke Constantine, his very large family, his mother and his brother. It was known as the *Mramorny Dvoretz*, i.e. 'Marble Palace', all pale grey veined with white.

Away from Palace Quay, to the right of Nicholas Bridge, stood the modest enough home of Grand-Duke Paul, Wladimir's brother. Just round the corner of the English Quay, along the banks of the Neva, you came on the great palace of the Emperor's sister, Grand-Duchess Xenia. I well remember the exquisite wrought-iron railings edging the garden in front.

Two more must be mentioned, and both were on Nevsky Prospect—the immense dark red Mariinsky Palace, the town home of the Dowager Empress, and further down, on the opposite side, a far less majestic palace belonging to young Grand-Duke Dimitry, Paul's only son. In 1914, when he went to the front, his palace became the Anglo-Russian Hospital for the war casualties.

All those palaces had their histories; all left their imprint on the city founded by their great ancestor. However chilly the state rooms of the Winter Palace, they were bone of St Petersburg's bone, and they witnessed to her proud imperial beginnings.

And so, in a wholly different way, were the city's dark corners, slummy alleys and lanes, where no sane person would venture after dark, where the solemn, black-coated policemen walked in pairs, their trained eyes piercing the shadows, their gauntleted hands ready to pounce on any transgressor of law and order.

There were all too many such corners in St Petersburg, but I knew very few of them. I walked down Grafsky Lane by daylight only, where the timid Tartar children peered at me through the dirty, curtained, narrow windows of the tenements and where shawled and veiled Tartar women slipped by, their hands clutching baskets, to the nearest and cheapest market. But Grafsky Lane was by no means the darkest corner of St Petersburg. There were dreadfully overcrowded tenements along Maly Boulevard on Vassily Island, hungry-looking hovels on the Islands to the north of St Petersburg where I saw two small boys fight over a few rotten turnips, tiny huts by the banks of the little Chernaya River (*Chernaya Riechka*) where a fisherman's children, ragged and bare-legged, watched their mother gut and clean two herrings for dinner. There were many more such. I heard of them but I did not see them all. What I do remember is that, in spite of penury and all it involved, it was very seldom that you would meet with grim despair. The poorest among the poor never lost their zest for life: singing and laughter could be heard at many a market place when, the day's business over, the unblessed folk would go in search of a half-rotten cabbage or a bunch of tired-looking carrots left under one stall or another. Just before a weekday sunset and on Sundays, gaiety gained in vigour with the sound of *garmoni-kas* and even common whistles. Any street those people lived in was their theatre and their kingdom.

There were tenements and to spare on Vassily Island, tiny flats of two or three rooms, a primitive kitchen included, peopled by minor civil servants for whom a bottle of cheap Crimean wine was an occasion to remember all through the year, who would describe an ordinary Easter card received from their superior in office over and over again, who were happy to get their daughters married with cabbage pasties and beer for the wedding breakfast. . . . And in their turn they were part of St Petersburg, inarticulately aware of her beauty, enduring her climatic vagaries, and heroically patient with her cobbled streets since they could not afford the daily tram fare to their offices.

St Petersburg could offer most varied amusements.

There was a place, its whereabouts having slipped from the memory, called the Luna Park, very modern, expensive, and considered 'fast', with a skating rink, a dance hall, a restaurant and electrically-run bumper cars whizzing round and round a large oval space ornamented with miniature orange trees in blue tubs, all of which I learned on hearsay. Scattered all over the South Bank were the fashionable *cafés-chantants* where people ate, drank, listened to modern songs and danced the tango and other dances which at the time would not have been tolerated in any private ballroom. Once, driving with my Aunt Nadine to Nicholas Station, we passed a young woman in a pink satin gown lavishly trimmed with fur, high-heeled satin slippers, and a curled pink feather pinned to her hair and falling down below her waist. I stared. My aunt turned away. The *vanka* said contemptuously:

'One of those *chantant* singers, I reckon! Who else would be wearing all that fur on a summer's day?'

I heard of all those places from grown-up cousins, Alexander, Boris and Natalie. 'They are rather fun—but vulgar, too.' I allowed for the fun and felt furious about the vulgarity. I sensed that it should have no place in St Petersburg.

But there were great theatres—the Mariinsky, all sapphire-blue within, for opera and ballet where, on one occasion, I saw Sedova in the Swan Lake. There was the Alexandrinsky for 'straight' plays, and the little Mikhailovsky, the so-called French theatre, where, on a happy day in January a wealthy cousin from the South took me to see Moliere's *Précieuses Ridicules*.

For people with lean purses, however, there was the great *Narodny Dom*, literally 'the People's House', built by the Emperor Nicholas II and opened by him in 1902. It stood on one of the islands on the North Bank of the Neva, a severe Grecian-looking building in pale grey stone. Factory hands, University students, minor civil servants and suchlike went there in their hundreds. Even the stalls and boxes were cheap; one did not have to wear grand clothes, and there was a restaurant where good and cheap food could be had. Nothing but soft drinks were served. The Narodny Dom was maintained by regular subsidies from the Emperor's privy purse.

There I went in 1909 to hear Glynka's opera, *A Life for the Tsar* with one of the greatest singers of the day, Maria Dolina, in the star role. Glynka set his theme in the early seventeenth

Glynka

century when the first Romanov, Michael, Peter the Great's grandfather, was elected Tsar by the National Assembly in Moscow. The Poles had their own candidate for the Russian throne and they sent a few of their nobles, accompanied by a troop of mounted soldiers, to the Ipatiev Abbey near Kostroma where Michael was staying. The Poles meant to lure him out and kill him. It happened in winter; they were caught in a blizzard and lost their way. Eventually they fetched up near a hamlet where a peasant, Ivan Soussanin, shrewd enough to guess their intention, offered to lead them to the Abbey. Instead, he brought them into the very heart of a wild impenetrable forest.

'Where have you brought us?' a Pole cried angrily.

'Where it was necessary—' replied Soussanin. 'You had hoped to find a traitor. No such live in my country.'

In their fury the Poles killed him, but Michael Romanov was saved.

An elder sister of my mother's, my Aunt Fanny, who mostly lived abroad and had made a name for herself by her Russian historical studies, knew Maria Dolina who, on hearing about my aunt's visit to St Petersburg, sent her three tickets for Glynka's great opera. The last call taken and the curtain fallen, we were about to leave when someone brought a message from Maria Dolina. She had never met my mother but she invited us three to supper. So we sat down again, my heart thudding with excitement.

Within a few minutes, the make-up off her face, wearing a plain grey woollen dress, plump and friendly, Dolina appeared and began kissing us all. We followed her to the restaurant where we supped off cabbage soup, mushroom patties and raspberry jelly. There was lemonade to drink. Dolina, I remember, was enchanted with her audience.

'It is good music they want, and they get it here!'

'And your voice—' put in my aunt, and Dolina laughed.

'Very kind of you! Oh! I have such a topsy-turvy week! Tomorrow I am singing at the Putilovsky steel works, the day after at someone's cotton mill up the Neva, and on Friday I shall be a great lady—driven in a special train to Tsarskoe Selo, eat my dinner with their Majesties, and then sing peasant songs to them. I hope they will be pleased.'

It was late when we left the Narodny Dom to catch the very last steamer to carry us back to Vassily Island. The steamer was crowded, and I lost sight of my mother and aunt as soon as we got on board. There was no moon, and the river was felt rather than seen, but there seemed no need to see all that beauty. It lived in the wind and in the air. We came alongside the Admiralty wharf, and the oil lamps flung their pallid gleam against the pale walls. We took off and glided on under the arches of Nicholas Bridge, and soon the steamer's engines stopped. I moved towards the little gangway, my mind full of Glynka, Dolina and the unseen beauty all round about me.

★

St Petersburg fairly teemed with 'places of enlightenment'. At the lowest level were the so called 'City Schools', free for all the poor people's children. Then came the *guymnasii* where modest fees were charged. Boys and girls from the middle class went there, children of minor civil servants, clergy and tradespeople. Then there were military schools where boys were prepared for the army, the Naval College and the so called *Corps de Pages* which occupied itself solely with the prospective candidates for guards regiments, the Lyceum which provided for the carefully chosen members of the diplomatic service, and many other places of 'higher' education—beginning with St Petersburg University founded by the Emperor Alexander I in 1819.

But for girls, educational facilities were very few. In my own day, the best private schools, like Koebkes' and Countess Litta's, charged terrific fees. The best boarding-schools, known as 'Institutes', were under Imperial protection and admitted none but the daughters of nobility and gentry.

The first of them was founded by Catherine the Great in 1764.

Well away from the centre of the city in what used to be an unpeopled wilderness, the Empress's architects built a huge house in Italianate style, all cream and pale blue, with a colonnade here and a colonnade there. It was the Smolny Institute, the very first of its kind in Russia. Pupils stayed for seven years and at first even their holidays were spent there, the great park behind the house affording enough space for exercise. The programme, laid down after the pattern of French convent schools, could not be said to shine educationally. ... The main idea was to turn out socially accomplished young ladies, not scholars. A pupil, having left this establishment, might not be certain whether Naples were in Italy or Spain, and believed the French to be wicked because they ate frogs. But she spoke French perfectly, could dance and play the harp and clavicord, knew how to embroider on silk and satin, how to enter and to leave a room and, finally, how to behave in the presence of Royalty.

The educational programme was certainly extended with the foundation of more and more Institutes. The pupils left these for home at Christmas, Easter and for the whole of the summer. The female members of the dynasty, in particular either dowager or reigning Empresses, continued to take a keen interest in these schools. But certain details, decreed by Catherine the Great, still remained in force. To the very end, i.e. till 1917, the girls went on wearing a uniform made to an eighteenth century

pattern. It consisted of a long and tremendously wide 'robe' of
fine cashmere, maroon for the juniors, powder blue for 'the
middle', and a rather ugly green for the seniors. The 'robe'
had a boned corsage, cut very low in front and at the back,
and ruched sleeves came down but a few inches below the
shoulder. Over the robe came a small white lawn apron, and
the bare arms were covered by white lawn sleeves. Over the
shoulders came a short cape of the same material. The pupils
wore thin shoes of black prunella and white stockings.

All the Institutes were housed in immense buildings; class-
rooms and dormitories were heated rather inadequately, and
didn't one shiver through the long wintry days!

Now, the very last of such Institutes was founded by Grand-
Duchess Xenia either in 1895 or 1896. It was housed in the
immense palace of Grand-Duke Peter, quite close to Nicholas
Bridge on the South Bank.

I can't now remember what connection my father had with
it; but I believe it had something to do with 'the higher education' for girls: 'Xeniinsky' as it came to be known, was the
only school of its kind to possess the so called 'superior courses'
where girls, having finished the seven years' programme, stayed
on studying both science and humanities.

And in August 1913 I found myself taken as a Grand-Ducal
pupil (my mother could never have afforded the fees) and
entered the Upper Third in a mood of intense rebellion. My
stay there was to last till May 1916—but I felt robbed of all my
liberties. The garden was big—but not big enough. The lessons
naturally included such abominations as geometry and physics,
and the masters we had made nothing interesting of the subjects
they taught.

We used to go home three times a year, but the start of every
holiday depended on our conduct marks. During my first term
I so distinguished myself that I left for Christmas five days later

than the rest and was told I could consider myself lucky not to be expelled.

It happened during a history lesson. The master was a retired artillery officer. He sat at his high dais, droning on and on about Henry VIII and his successors. Suddenly I heard him say:

'Henry had one son, who reigned as Edward VI, whose mother was the unfortunate Anne Boleyn.'

He paused and I shot up from my desk.

'I am sorry—but Edward VI's mother was Jane Seymour!'

The *dame de classe*, always present at every lesson 'to observe proprieties' gasped. So did the girls. The master did not. His face gone an angry red, he barked at me:

'Sit down.'

I did, conscious of the enormity but quite unashamed of it. There followed an uncomfortable interview with the Head. To correct a master during a lesson was terrible, she told me.

'But he doesn't know enough History to teach it,' I stammered.

My next performance could indeed have led to expulsion.

During the last term of every year, all the masters, the Head and her two assistants, one male and the other female, sat in council behind closed doors to discuss all of us, our progress or otherwise. When I moved into the Upper Second, our classroom adjoined the great white hall where such conclaves were held. Now all the doors of Xeniinsky were double, i.e. with enough room for two or three people to stand in the space between, and the key-holes were enormous. I suggested to two girls that it would be rather fun to listen to some home-truths about ourselves. One girl backed out—she was rather scared. But the other fell in with my idea. She was the daughter of a Russian ambassador somewhere.

Well, by dint of much cunning, we succeeded in hiding ourselves just in time. We could hear everything perfectly. The

start was rather dull—the report being given by the mathematics master who had nothing good to say of either of us but,
as we knew that already, it did not particularly interest us.

There followed a rather spicy spell. Physics and cosmography
were taught by our he-head, and his sarcastic remarks about the
papers I produced were most entertaining.

My friend's surname began with a G. I came before her.
We listened with bated breath.

'As Inspector,' he began in his clipped copper-and-steel voice,
'it was my business to read all through the reports. I see that
Mademoiselle Almedingen has the highest marks for History
and Literature; and there it ends. The French master says her
grammar is deplorable. The geography report would be comi-
cal if it were not tragic. As to the rest. . . .' he paused. 'I tell you,
ladies and gentlemen, that pupil is a fraud. She has an excep-
tional memory and trades on what crumbs she has picked up. I
for one would not rate her intelligence at all high and—'

Just then he was interrupted most disastrously.

Being hardly ever used, the space between the doors was
exceedingly dusty. My poor friend sneezed so loudly that every
other sound was drowned in it, and she sneezed again. It was
only a matter of seconds before the doors were flung open, and
there we stood, our white lawn accessories most lamentably
dusty.

'Ah—' said the Inspector.

There followed no comment. Under the guard of a silent
but most obviously scandalized *dame de classe* we were taken
to the farthest wing of the great palace, to the infirmary which
on certain occasions served as a house of detention. A harassed
matron rushed towards us.

'Have they got a cold? Are they sickening for measles?'

'Far worse—' replied the *dame de classe*, and we were put
into separate rooms, the key turned in each door. The window

of my prison gave me a lovely view of Nicholas Bridge and the busy waterfront of Vassily Island. I laid my elbows on the window-sill and stared hungrily. I had not a shred of doubt that I would be expelled with ignominy.

The key was turned at last, and a very timid maid slipped into my room with the supper tray, laid it on the table, and vanished silently. Under the plate of rather tepid macaroni smothered in tomato sauce lay a note from my friend.

'Don't worry. They can't expel you and not me, and if they expelled me, Papa is certain to make a fuss.'

She proved right. Much later I would learn that expulsion had been suggested, but the Head, the late Princess Eugenie Golitzin, who was my mother's cousin, had pointed out that to expel me and not Tatiana G. would have been a gross injustice.

'And if we expel Tatiana, there is certain to be trouble with the Dowager Empress.'

A fortnight of our summer holiday was docked off, but in the eyes of other pupils both of us were heroines, and during my last three terms the Inspector's sarcasm lost its sting for me.

In May 1916 we were 'out', and few, if any, of us knew that by May 1917 Xeniinsky would exist no longer. By 1920 the building became 'the Palace of Labour' but I have no idea what the 'Labour' consisted of. Anyway, the great forecourt was closed to all outsiders.

The Institute's traditions, uniform and way of life may well have been archaic in the twentieth century. But its discipline was good both for the mind and the body. Our masters may not have been brilliant but at least they did not report minor breaches of the rule. The mathematics master had a habit of wandering up and down the classroom; more than once he would find me absorbed in some history book, and he never reported me. 'Mommsen,' he muttered, leaning over my desk,

'Well, I suppose ancient Rome says more to you than Euclid.'

As to the body, we were never sent to the infirmary because of a slight cold or a headache. It was in a way part of our training, to endure the cold and the heat and the occasional aches and pains without mentioning them to anyone. And all our dormitories were on the third floor. The windows faced a corner of St Petersburg I had known and loved since my early childhood, and that was a greater comfort than I deserved at the time.

CHAPTER NINE

Shopping—Real and Imaginary

THE LAST kind was far more thrilling than the first in that it opened the door to endless adventures and to variations of the Grimm story about a purse which never went empty even when the apparently last coin was taken out of it.

The centre of many among those adventures was Nevsky Prospect. In the quality of its wares it could well be compared with Bond Street or Fifth Avenue. It was supposed to be the longest and widest street in the world; it stretched for about five miles from Alexander Gardens to the Moscow Gate, beyond Alexander Nevsky Abbey. Laid out about 1706 by the Swedish prisoners of war, the Prospect was the heartbeat of

St Petersburg. Its pavements were so broad that twelve or more people walking abreast would not have been crowded.

It had a few churches, the Kazan Cathedral, two palaces, the tall-towered City Hall, the dark red massif of the Imperial Library, several banks and offices, but its shops reigned over them all. They were expensive. There was a story about a

The Kazan Cathedral

Cabinet Minister's wife who spent the whole of her husband's salary and that in the course of a single morning by visiting only three shops.

They were all familiar to me—mostly from the outside and especially during the winter months when the brief hours of daylight put a stop to the walks further afield.

Window shopping was an exquisite pleasure. I would run

across Alexander Gardens and cross to the right side of Nevsky Prospect, and soon reached the first halt in front of the huge windows of Alexandre's, a twin to Tiffany and Asprey. There I would feast my eyes on the display of odds and ends of tooled leather, malachite, jade and ivory; on umbrellas, walking sticks, purses, bags and multi-coloured scarves woven of Persian silk. No price tickets could be seen, but that did not prevent me from making one imaginary purchase after another, and choosing incredible Christmas presents for everybody I knew in my small orbit, beginning with my mother whose birthday fell on Christmas Day.

Once only did I venture to enter the great doorway. It happened in the summer of 1914. I was sixteen at the time and earning a little money by daily teaching English to the wooden-minded daughter of a linen-king. The lesson lasted three hours, and the man paid me fifteen roubles a month, just under thirty shillings in our money, yet it seemed high fortune to me.

I got to the house on Fontanka Quay at nine in the morning, and my thin, pale-lipped pupil waited for me in a room which was softly cushioned but too thickly carpeted and airless for me. She was about three years younger than me but she looked bored enough for a jaded woman of forty. We struggled with a brief translation for something like an hour; then she would read a page of a book her father had bought for her at Watkins', the English bookshop. I remember its title: *The Coming of Arthur*, but I am not at all sure if Arthur ever did come— until the very end which we never reached.

Precisely at 10.30 a most superior maid, all white frills and starched skirts, brought in a tray with a silver pot of chocolate and a plateful of home-made croissants. My pupil had nothing, but she urged me to eat and drink, and that daily treat was certainly welcome. The tray removed, I would start on a spell of conversation, but Mania said:

'I have had more than enough. Let us talk in Russian. I am tired of English.'

The first time it happened I retorted:

'I am here to teach you English. If you are tired, I'd better go.'

She said quickly.

'You can't. You must stay till twelve and it is just eleven. I know Papa pays you for three hours.'

Well, I could not escape the feeling that I was treated more or less as if I were a fly on the ceiling. Many a time I met my pupil's mother in the passage and she always ignored me. Some mornings I got to the house only to be told that the young lady was just about to go for a drive or that she did not feel well enough to have her lesson. The portly butler delivered the message and closed the door before I could ask, 'Am I expected to come tomorrow?'

Once my pupil flatly refused either to take a dictation or to translate. For one thing, she expected her dressmaker 'at any moment', and for another she was all agog to show me what her mother had bought for her the day before. I looked at the expensive oddments of tortoiseshell and ivory and said:

'I suppose you got these from some place in Nevsky Prospect?'

'Yes—at Alexandre's.'

'I shop there too—mostly in the winter.'

She stared at me.

'In my imagination—' I explained hurriedly—'I just stand at a window and I see something really beautiful, and I enjoy looking at it—so it is mine—in a way.'

She looked at me rather oddly and said nothing, but when the first month ended, it was the starched, befrilled maid who opened the door, handed me an envelope, and delivered a verbal message that her young lady would soon be going away and my services were no longer required. I was not sorry.

Never before had I had fifteen roubles in my pocket and I felt most beautifully reckless. On my way home, I entered Alexandre's and bought a black morocco purse for my mother. Exactly two roubles left out of fifteen, I hurried home, that first and last purchase at Alexandre's anything but a minor triumph.

Past Alexandre's were the small ground-floor windows of Druce's, the famous *Magasin Anglais* where they sold Harris tweeds, English soap, gloves and hose. Every article was imported and consequently expensive. Beyond was Cabassue's, small and sharply select with its French gloves, ties and handherchiefs; a little further on Knopf's, a minor replica of Alexandre's, and then the Mecca of all my desires—Wolff's great bookshop where it was possible to buy books, magazines and papers in seven languages. The men and women behind the counters were most kindly people: they never minded anyone leafing a book or a magazine and then going out, not having made a single purchase. I did not dare to do it very often, though. Close to Wolff's stood a most entrancing map shop, the display of its three large windows teaching me more geography than all the textbooks together.

The other side of Nevsky Prospect had different attractions: Kornilov's with its show of porcelain; the jewelled splendours of Fabergé; the fragrance that poured out every time someone opened Brocard's door where they sold French soap and scents; the discreet elegance of Scipion's, a few pairs of delicately coloured suède gloves arranged on black velvet; the little windows of Abrikossov's set out with biscuits, salami and boxes of fruit sweets. There I lingered seldom enough, nor do I remember spending much time at the windows of *Aux Gourmets*, the foremost French confectioners in St Petersburg, or in front of the huge windows of Elisseev Brothers, the most important and expensive grocers in the whole of the country. Squeezed between a most uninteresting hat shop and an equally dull German shoe shop were four booksellers and stationers, far less exclusive than Wolff's but just as attractive. Having chosen an imaginary library I would cross the Prospect again towards the Town Hall and study the beehive busyness of *Gostiny Dvor*, an immense two-storied building, its four sides occupying about a square mile. Literally translated, *Gostiny Dvor* means 'Merchants' Yard'. The ground-floor shops were drapers, hat and shoe shops, and all followed the rigid custom of Nevsky Prospect: 'prix-fixe'. Prices were less dizzy than, say, at Cabassue, but all bargaining was barred. I still remember one draper's window with its cascade of velvet arranged in a rainbow pattern and a shoe shop with a display of ladies' boots and shoes in every shade of violet. Here and there I saw boldly printed notices in three languages, but I doubt if many foreign residents in St Petersburg shopped at *Gostiny Dvor*. Even the ground floor was unmistakably Russian.

As to the first floor, it was the Nijny Novgorod fair in little, and the real fun started along its rows of shops which sold ready-made clothes, cheap shoes, furs, carpets and rather clumsy furniture. There my mother took me to choose a winter coat. A woman came forward and put it on me. It certainly fitted. A man appeared and mentioned the price. My mother shook her head and made for the door. The man followed us, lowering the price with each step he took. At last, he sighed. 'Have it your way, Madam—' and we turned back and bought the coat at the price mentioned by my mother. Yet sometimes a customer's bluff would be called. One May morning we went to *Gostiny Dvor* because I needed some canvas shoes. The man said:

'Forty copeks a pair, Madam, and cheap at that! Down below they would be sixty.'

'Perhaps,' replied my mother, 'but I usually pay fifty for two pairs.'

We left the shop but the man did not follow. In the end I got my canvas shoes at a small shop on Vassily Island where a fat old woman asked forty copeks and let us have the two pairs for thirty.

The elegant shops up and down Nevsky Prospect knew nothing about such chaffering. They did not even exhibit the notice 'Fixed prices' either in their windows or inside. In fact, the price of any article seemed something too indelicate to be mentioned until the article had been definitely chosen. Then the black-gowned assistant would murmur scarcely above the rustle of tissue paper: 'That will be twenty-five roubles, Madam—' and the lady in silks and furs would fumble with the clasp of her bag and put the gold pieces on the counter. I saw it happen during my first and last visit to Alexandre's when one such woman chose a pigskin notebook.

I do not remember nursing any particular interest in food and delicatessen shops, but there were a few exceptions. One was Filippov's great bakery on Nevsky Prospect, below the Imperial Library. They were kings among bakers, one of the very few really great Russian shops in the city. They used wheat, rye, barley and oat flour, and I once heard that they made nearly fifty kinds of bread—both loaves and rolls of most fantastic shapes. Just before Palm Sunday it was the fashion to go to Filippov's to buy their famous *zhavoronky* (*zhavoronok* means 'lark'), little wheaten rolls, shaped precisely like the birds, sweetened and slightly spiced with saffron, with two tiny currants for eyes. The whole year round they sold patties, those delectable *piroshki*, as hot as hot, made much in the way of a doughnut but thinner, and triangular in shape. The price varied according to the contents from two to five copeks, but even a couple of them made a meal.

To get them meant making for the cashier's desk, handing the money and receiving a small orange chit with the amount written very clearly. Armed with it, I would turn to the counter and think it fortunate if there happened to be a queue: it gave me time to make up my mind. I believe there were more than twenty kinds to choose from—each more delectable than the others—meat, chicken, game, fish, egg, mushroom, carrot, onion, cabbage, apple, and several kinds of jam. The patties were handed over, half covered by thin brown paper, and people ate them then and there. There were neither tables nor chairs, but I remember many white-aproned boys, brooms in their hands, weaving their way in among the customers and sweeping up crumbs and discarded bits of brown paper, into oddly shaped green containers. Filippov's, apart from their bread deliveries, was not patronized by 'grand folk', and when I went to Xeniinsky in 1913, the girls were horrified when I told them how often I had enjoyed those patties.

'But someone said you can't even sit down there!' cried one.

'And all the shop assistants and clerks crowd the place!' cried another.

'I suppose so—' I told them, 'but the patties were good and the crowd most interesting to watch—' which was hardly a fortunate remark to make at such a school.

Then there was the French *confiserie*, Berrin's, in Morskaya Street, I think, just off the Nevsky Prospect. It was wholly out of our financial orbit: even its tiny sponge cakes cost the earth, but on one or two occasions I was invited there, and I remember the ices served in tall slim glasses by an alarmingly elegant Frenchwoman.

Away from Nevsky Prospect, behind St Isaac's Cathedral, in a very quiet street was a house-linen and underwear shop kept by some sectarian philanthropic society. We did not go there oftener than once a year or so, but how well I remember the plump elderly women in starched grey and white print dresses, their hair gathered up into a bun, standing behind a wide

counter and talking about 'salvation' so earnestly that, when I
was little, I wondered about a possible link between cotton
pillow cases and 'salvation'.

In Gogol Street was the famous Chistiakov dairy which
again meant an annual visit just before Easter: Chistiakov's sold
the finest eggs in the city. I can still see the large tubs of dark

yellow Siberian butter, the enormous round cheeses, and the rough brown-red earthenware pots containing *smetana*, a kind of thick cream used for making an Easter dainty. But the white-aproned men, who served you so briskly and politely, spoke an oddly accented Russian. They were all *chukhna*, peasants from the Baltic Provinces, and an egg, which is neuter in Russian (*yaizo*) became a 'he' the way they pronounced it. The men made a most fascinating mixture of 'much' and 'many'.

A few doors away was Stoll and Schmidt, the cheapest and foremost chemists of St Petersburg, where all the assistants were German with the exception of a young Spaniard employed chiefly for his knowledge of French.

'He massacres it—' my mother remarked to me once. 'I prefer to be served by a German.'

Somehow that huge place reminded me of a station waiting-room. In the very middle of the vast interior stood a column reaching right up to the ceiling and a deep leather-covered seat was all round it. There I would sit whilst my mother went to a counter for cod-liver oil, mothballs and suchlike. I sat in the tantilizing scents of pepper, camphor and various spices, and was able to travel east and west in my mind.

And there was Peto's, the children's paradise. It stood in a narrow street, whose name escapes me, and occupied three or four small humpy houses. There was not a hint of any window dressing. Once within, I just rambled from one little room to another, all crammed with toys, children's books, children's stationery in blue and pink, boxes of water-colours and crayons, and masses of multicoloured trifles, mostly made of cardboard and covered with gold or silver foil, to hang on a Christmas tree—baskets, carriages, animals, houses, violins and fishes. In spring Peto's had a fine collection of Easter eggs made of china, wood and cardboard, of all colours and sizes.

I believe the proprietor was French, but I never saw him.

All the assistants were middle-aged German women who massacred Russian and French with an equal ease and spared no trouble in helping a child to lay out its money to the best advantage. Peto's was not grand. Its goods were excellent but the prices were low.

'An animal book, my dear, with pictures—see—all in colour —lions, tigers, leopards. How much can you spend? Now let me see—yes—twenty copeks, I am afraid, and you have just fifteen! Oh dear! Well, here is a smaller one costing twelve, but I am sorry, you would not find a leopard there. Will that do? If not and if your Mamma does not mind waiting, I might find something else for you!'

I never thought of them as shop assistants. They were just so many kindly maiden aunts. They would take the same trouble with a child like myself as with an elegant little creature, driven to their door in a private carriage and so obviously proud of her ermine muff.

When I was about eight, in the summer of 1906, I discovered yet another little paradise—all on my own, too! Two second-hand book-barrows on the 6th Line of Vassily Island. They belonged to two seedy, weedy-looking brothers, whose grey ravelled beards and patched-up coats of yellow alpaca rather suggested Hans Andersen's stories. The barrows were crammed with second-hand books, mostly English and Tauchnitz editions, all of them probably discarded by the English living on the Island. The books were tattered but incredibly cheap, and in rainy weather the brothers spread a very ancient piece of tarpaulin over the barrows.

There, one blissful morning in June, I enlarged my little library by *Huckleberry Finn*, *The Wide Wide World*, *Daisy Chain*, *East Lynne*, and two or three others. The brothers smiled and said in unison:

'Six copeks for the lot won't be too much for you, little lady?'

Later, with clearer ideas about financial values and prices, I wondered how the old men managed to earn a livelihood.

*

There was yet another such paradise much bigger and more tempting in Wladimir Avenue on the South Bank. The whole of that wide long street was occupied by antique and second-hand bookshops. The latter had stalls outside, and much of my pocket money was spent there. At any such stall you could pick up a book for one or two coppers, and the odd thing was that those in charge of the stalls were illiterate. With one exception, and that man was one of the most lovable oddities in St Petersburg.

He was a retired schoolmaster, a small, fussy, bearded man, shabbily but neatly dressed. He would help customers to choose their purchases, often shaking his head at a particular choice. Homer and Virgil were his twin passions. He introduced me to both, and looked horrified when I told him I knew no Greek and very little Latin.

'So you walk in darkness—' he said sharply and began reciting a piece of the *Iliad*, quite unconcerned about the customers crowding about the stall.

Homer and Virgil apart, I did buy quite a few books from him. Little by little we became friendly and then the little man climbed from literary heights to the pedestrian level of food.

'Do you eat onions?' he flung at me.

'Sometimes.'

'And fish?'

'Yes—'

'Listen to me—' he leant across the stall and his voice was very solemn .'If you want to make the best use of your mind, eat nothing except fish and onions. They alone nurture and expand the mind. No other food does that. Never touch meat or poultry. Never be tempted by anything sweet. I drink my tea without sugar, and I have lived on fish and onions all my life—boiled, mind you! Frying destroys their virtue. Will you remember?'

'Yes—' I said and tendered the coppers for a battered copy of Racine's *Tragedies*. Just as I was about to turn away, a not-too-young girl in a carefully patched print gown came up to the stall.

'Here is your dinner, Dad,' she said, put down two plates, took off the napkin and I could not help seeing a substantial slice of meat pie cushioned on a pile of fried potatoes on one plate, and a generous portion of baked vermicelli pudding on the other. I moved away rather hurriedly, and the woman caught up with me.

'I expect he held forth about his boiled fish and onions?' she asked.

I nodded. She went on conversationally:

'He is not a liar, you know. He read something like that in one of his books, and it sort of became something *he* had done. Mother and I have had that fish and onions talk for nearly two months now, and before that we'd heard that tea was poisonous —though Dad went on drinking his two glasses three times a day. I wonder what will happen next!'

'He was a schoolmaster, wasn't he?'

'And such a scholar too—' pride rang in her voice. 'But he lost his job years ago. . . .' she sighed, 'and he gets no pension. Well, Mother and I manage with the sewing we take in. And there is the bookstall—in the summer, that is. They won't have him inside the shop.'

I hesitated before asking:

'Why did he lose his job?'

'Well, he taught Latin and Greek and suchlike, and was so

good at it, and the Ministry sent a most difficult inspector as examiner. The man knew science, I think, and nothing else, and Dad said he was a fraud. That was enough! You can't say such things to superiors,' and she sighed again. 'But Dad meant no harm. He is far too honest—'

Next time I went to that bookstall, I knew I was going to meet a friend. Fish and onions were forgotten. He talked of nothing except the blessing of telephones, and I felt that he knew that I must have known he could never afford such a luxury, but we did not mention anything as vulgar as money or its lack.

*

There were many markets up and down the city, but they mostly sold vegetables, fruit, dairy produce, meat and fish, with an occasional 'junk' stall here and there where invalidish-looking chairs huddled cheek by jowl with cracked pieces of china and rusty ironmongery. St Andrew's Market on Vassily Island was the smallest of those markets and the one I knew best, though I was not allowed to go there by myself until I had reached my early teens. It was there that I saw something incredible on a 'junk' stall—a thick pile of blank copybooks.

'How much?' I asked, my voice unsteady, and the elderly woman hugged her huge scarlet shawl and said sourly:

'That rubbish? Take the lot for three copeks if you want to! I shall be glad to get rid of them. They weigh so heavy and nobody wants them.'

I certainly did. There were fifteen of them, and my incessant 'scribbling' was most happily assured for a whole year.

With one exception, prices of all home products were low. Clothes, shoes, furniture, stationery and food cost little enough. Particularly food—with one startling exception. I remember one of my tutors, a shabby, hungry-looking university student, who told me that for twenty copeks (less that 5d), he could get a decent meal at the college canteen.

They give you nourishing soup, meat or fish, vegetables and a jam tart. As much bread as you want! he added wistfully: 'But I can only afford it about once a week,' and, to my startled 'why?' he answered: 'Because even twenty copeks makes a hole in my budget, young lady. I get fifteen roubles (about thirty shillings in English money) a month from my father, and I earn the rest but it does not go very far.' Yet food was cheap; the foremost hostelry in the city, *l'Hôtel de Europe*, charged one rouble and twenty-five copeks for a three course luncheon, about 2/6d in our money. People with a budget as modest as ours was, would spend two roubles (four shillings) a week on food, and they did not starve. In weight, the Russian lb. was two or three ounces less than ours. In actual value, it stood much higher, with sugar less than a penny a lb., dairy butter at 4d and sometimes less, eggs at 3d per ten. Meat and fish were equally cheap.

But there was one exception, caviar. Vassily Island did not sell it. You had to go to the South Bank to buy it.

Pressed caviar cost between eight and ten roubles a pound. The fresh kind was even dearer, and never once did I taste it in Russia. It was a wholly national product, and its high price may have been due to the vast quantities exported abroad.

But even those who could never afford it liked telling stories about caviar. There was one where a bank director had an exceptionally mean and rude wife. One New Year's day, always a great holiday in Russia, the man decided to give a party to all his employees down to the least important clerks. 'And see to it that there is enough caviar for everybody,' he told his wife.

The woman was mean but she liked playing the part of a

lady bountiful. She singled out the youngest and shabbiest among the clerks who seemed glued to his chair in a corner, a small table beside him. She swooped down on him and saw a plate heaped up with caviar on the table. The youth hurriedly put down his fork and got up. The woman remembered that she was hostess, reined in her indignation, and asked:

'Is everything all right?'

'Oh yes, Madam,' he stammered, 'why I feel quite at home—'

She snapped at him: 'How extraordinary. You would hardly eat caviar by the plateful in your own home!'

But if things were cheap, all imported articles were prohibitive, so high were the custom dues. I remember that a tablet of English soap cost nearly four times more than the home-made product. Russian porcelain was dear enough, but the prices charged for the smallest pieces of Dresden, Sèvres or Spode were fantastic. On my ninth birthday, in 1907, I first met with the severity of custom officials. From Rome my Aunt Helen had written that she was sending me a fringed sash made of crimson Italian silk. The parcel was brought to us not by a postman but by a grim-looking customs officer, and my mother at once said that she could not afford to pay the duty.

'Madam,' said the man, 'you would have to pay much more for such an article at any shop on Nevsky Prospect.'

'But I would never dream of buying any such thing—' she told him.

So the parcel was taken away. I suppose the Customs people later sold it at one of their auctions.

Wages, as I came to learn later, were wickedly low, and not everybody found work in St Petersburg. There was a Domestic Agency in a dim grey house in Basseynaya Street, not very far from Nicholas Station, where my mother used to go to engage servants. For one mistress in search of a cook or a maid, there would be over twenty applicants, most of them fresh-faced peasant girls from the depths of the country, come to St Petersburg because to them it was 'foreign' and the wage offered was certainly much higher than they would have got in the country. Some of those girls were illiterate but all carried references from their parish priests.

Once away from the elegance of the South Side, it was impossible either to enter or to leave a shop without seeing a beggar by the door. The police did not interfere so long as the beggars did not 'importune', but to hold out a palm and murmur almost inaudibly 'a copper for Christ's sake' ('*Khrista rady*'), did not amount to an offence—at least—not in the less fashionable parts of the capital. Beggars haunted markets, sat on the steps of church porches, and wandered up and down such of the streets as were not forbidden to them. Most of them were old and many honestly destitute, but quite a few considered beggardom as a legitimate source of income. I remember being told about an old woman who spent years and years near the porch of one of the lesser known churches on Vassily Island, and had her 'home' in a corner of a basement cubby-hole in some slummy alley near Maly Boulevard. When she died, the police found a sizable fortune hidden in her pallet. Since no relatives of hers were known to exist, the money was distributed to various charities.

St Nicholas' Cathedral

CHAPTER TEN

Piety in Marble and Granite

'COSMOPOLITAN, German, anyhow foreign—' such was the verdict passed on the city by many who had gone to work there, their own home towns sometimes more than a thousand miles away and even as far as over the Siberian border.

Cosmopolitan St Petersburg was—within certain limits—but not German and that in spite of great numbers of Germans settled there with their shops and offices. Hers was a different identity most peculiarly her very own. The great river and the magnificent quays were so many fragments of an unwritten saga. When, as happened so often, the wind freshened, the skies changed their blue for dark grey, and the Neva's broad stream ran a menacing black, you felt, as it were, drawn back to the beginnings, not of the city and not even of the humble fishing hamlets once scattered over the islands—but to far older origins. An ancient and sharply northern impress lay on St Petersburg, and all her waters confirmed it.

There was an elderly fisherman on the banks of Chernaya River to the north-east of Vassily Island. In between gutting and cleaning a few herrings and roach and grumbling about a grand-daughter who thought so much of dancing and too little of housework, he once told me a legend where the past and the present seemed to be woven together.

There was a savage war between water and dry land. Water was greedy and longed to extend its dominion over land, which was marshy and weak and had no strength to withstand the assault. Water was about to conquer the marshes when suddenly great rocks and boulders fell upon the marshes, and water had to recede.

'When did it all happen?' I asked, and he mumbled:

'Ah—there was no reckoning of time then.'

'But we have had bad floods—' I insisted. 'There was one when I was very small, about four I think, and our courtyard got flooded and there was neither milk nor bread for breakfast—'

'Ah,' he muttered, leaning over the fish, 'what does a single flood matter?'

I never knew where that legend had come from, but to me it explained a little of St Petersburg's magic.

Now, Peter the Great's Empire was Greek Orthodox. In Moscow, Tver, Kiev, Wladimir, Souzdal and any other ancient cities it was always churches with their onion-shaped cupolas and belfries that stood to the foreground, and few were the villages without an abbey or a convent in the background. Peter himself conformed to the old tradition when he laid the foundation-stone of St Samson's Church in his new capital. In my childhood, St Petersburg, though unable to outrival Moscow with its sixteen hundred sanctuaries, was rich enough in cathedrals and churches, some having been built by foreigners of genius.

Exquisitely sited, majestic with their great colonnaded porches of black marble, violet-veined granite and porphyry, they certainly added to the beauty of the capital, but somehow, with few exceptions, they failed to capture the warmth of Russia's ancient sanctuaries. Their sacristies were crowded with treasures rarely, if ever, shown to the public. Great artists had covered many of their walls with fine mosaics. The services were as perfect as the most ardent lover of liturgies could desire, and some of the choirs were justly famous. Nevertheless, few could be called sanctuaries in the deepest sense of the word. Even a village church, however poor and even ugly, had that quality—for all the shoddiness of the priests' vestments, the poverty of the altar appointments, and the sorry performance of the choir.

To give but a few examples of the pious splendours of St Petersburg there was the great cathedral of SS. Peter and Paul on the North Bank of the Neva. In bald terms, it was first and foremost the Imperial mausoleum. All the Romanovs with their wives and children lay there—with the exception of Peter II, the great founder's grandson who died in Moscow and was buried there. Parties of schoolchildren would be taken there and marshalled from one white marble sarcophagus to another, their teachers talking in rather studiedly subdued voices since, after all, they were in a cathedral and not in a museum. Soldiers of the so called Golden Company (*Zolotaya Rota*), resplendent in their scarlet and gold, stood on guard here and there. Groups of foreign tourists, companioned by interpreters whose linguistic abilities were rather peculiar, went from one great tomb to another, and I could not help wondering whether they gleaned much, if any, historical knowledge from the crumbs dispensed by their guides, one of whom said in broken English: 'Here is our Empress Elizabeth who lived parallel with your Queen Elizabeth—but they never met together—our Empress disliking voyages so muchly,' and I heard a quickly smothered laugh as an Englishwoman pointed the dates to her husband, the Empress Elizabeth having died in 1761!

Numberless wax candles were burning all over the place, and pale blue spirals of incense could be seen here and there, but it was impossible to escape the feeling of being in the company of curious sightseers, not devout worshippers.

St Isaac's on the South Bank was a marvel of loveliness with its colonnaded wings and its five great cupolas. It held the place of ecclesiastical pre-eminence in St Petersburg, and it had the largest chapter of all the cathedrals. Its congregation was said to be immense on Sundays and great feasts, particularly on Easter Eve when women put on their finest jewellery and ball-dresses for the midnight service, the so-called *Zautrenia*, but it was little more than a piously social gathering. I shall never forget the sense of shock I had when, once, window-shopping on Nevsky Prospect, I heard one elegant woman say to another:

'Now that Madam Aline has let me down I can't possibly go to the *Zautrenia*. I have nothing fit to wear.'

On weekdays, however, that vast, deserted interior carried its own compulsion. At the end of one of the wide aisles there was a great painting of Christ the King. I forget the artist's name, but not once did I reach that corner without seeing two or three people deep in prayer, the light of countless waxen candles adding splendour to the red and blue robes of Christ.

The great national sanctuary was Alexander Abbey at the far end of Nevsky Prospect, with its several churches, its fashionable cemetery, and the resplendent shrine of Prince Alexander of Novgorod, 'patron and protector of our city', as Peter the Great called him. But my memories of it are rather blurred. All I do remember is the humble grave of Fieldmarshal Suvorov in one of the cloisters.

For the great civic and national occasions the Kazan Cathedral was used. The Te Deums sung there were often attended by the Emperor, other members of the Imperial family, the Government, and numbers of important civil servants, as well as by a crowd of generals and admirals. On such occasions, many mounted gendarmes patrolled up and down Nevsky Prospect, and numbers of policemen cordoned off the little garden in front of the Cathedral. St Petersburg's municipality rode in black and grey coaches and nobody could gain admittance unless they had tickets. The service over, all the Kazan bells came to life, and the clergy, looking all the more portly in their heavy brocade vestments, appeared in the great porch and took their places, one gold and silver row facing the other, thus to bid God-speed to members of the Imperial family and others among the important worshippers.

That was the sign for the police cordon to get tighter. It would have been impossible to try and get across. From the opposite side the great cross and the robes of the clergy looked like so many overgrown daffodils, and on a sunny day the bejewelled mitres worn by some of the priests shone like some fantastic stars set in a fantastic sky.

Presently, carriages began moving towards the porch, and

the bells rose to a crescendo as though the very belfry were pleased to see the last of the important worshippers. With the last carriage gone, the bells began ringing down and before you knew where you were, the Prospect wore its habitual secular face. The gendarmes galloped away. The police dispersed, the expressions on their faces suggesting a relief that the arduous duty was over. The day's traffic began to flow down the ordinary channel. *Droshky* and *likhachy* drove past. People walked, talked, chatted with one another, and many, having glanced at a clock, vanished through the doors of the fashionable 'Quissisana' restaurant to refresh themselves with a plate of caviar or salmon sandwiches and a bottle of Crimean wine. Crowds of shop assistants and clerks, glad of the break in routine, strolled back to their desks and counters.

Yet such were rather widely spaced occasions. On ordinary days I seldom passed Kazan Cathedral without going in if but to see Kutuzov's tomb and to be once more reminded of the perils and the glories of 1812 as I looked at the bullet-riddled standards hanging above the humble gravestone.

Those were the main sanctuaries of St Petersburg, with piety expressed in terms of marble, granite and porphyry.

Yet there were exceptions, and first among them was St Andrew's Cathedral on Vassily Island, the spiritual home of all the Russian merchantry in the city. It was not particularly beautiful. It neighboured a noisy and noisome market. Its choir could not be said to be famous. Its bells were not outstandingly tuneful. But it was an anchorage for the homeless and the truly poor. It was never closed by night, and there were stoves, fed by logs, in some of the corners. The nearest Western comparison I can think of is St Martin-in-the-Fields in London. Under the shadow of St Andrew's honest penury shed all the shame attributed to it by social dogmatists and became a stark simplicity in full accord with the life of the Master.

What Russian merchants settled in St Petersburg remained truly Russian in their benevolence and generosity. They helped hospitals, they founded almshouses, they took many a widow under their wing, and none of it was done in the chilly name of official charity. The Russian merchantry of St Petersburg helped the real poor from no sense of duty but because of true charity. I would often see their wives go to Sunday Mass at St Andrew's, accompanied either by their daughters or their maids carrying heavy satchels. Loaves of bread, meat pies, fruit pies, vegetables and home-made sausages were distributed in the porch—together with many a copper coin—none of the gifts soured by a sense of compulsory almsgiving but sweetened by kind-heartedness. Some among the beggars were cheats, but that meant nothing to the merchants' wives. They gave of their abundance unconditionally and that made any gift perfect in loveliness.

Sometimes, on a weekday afternoon, I would slip into St Andrew's. There was nothing beautiful to see there, and I knew that it belonged to old Moscow rather than to St Petersburg. None the less, it was satisfying. True charity stepped up and down the nave and the twin aisles, and sang its song—far lovelier than any anthem performed by the most skilful choir. The atmosphere of St Andrew's reconciled you to so much— the slums of Vassily Island and elsewhere, the chilliness of the great cathedrals, the unending daily struggles of so many denizens of the city.

But St Andrew's Cathedral was by no means the only exception.

When we lived in a corner house of Nicholas Quay and the 14th Line, we had a 'cell' of the Kiev Abbey just opposite. Now that Abbey was one of the most famous in the whole of the old Russian Empire. It had produced saints, theologians and mystics without number. The cell in St Petersburg was a very small one—a one-storied house affording enough room for about ten monks and a tiny dim chapel where anyone could go at any time of day or night, touch a bell button, and tell the monk on duty that they wanted a Te Deum or a requiem. He would bow, suggest a time, ask for the name and address, and vanish.

That tiny dim chapel was a reconciling place. In a way I can't explain it succeeded in linking St Petersburg to the rest of Russia. It was sharply alive to all the moods of the Neva. Equally, it brought you close to all the great waters and lakes of old Russia. Timelessness breathed from those low walls covered with mosaics you could hardly see in the flickering candlelight. Some four or five monks came out to sing a Te Deum or a requiem, and their voices joined in the timelessness. The echo of the last 'Amen' still lingering in the small place, you knew you were alone, and not quite alone. The pagan beginnings of the nineteen islands and the new dispensation seemed to be most strangely but satisfyingly at one.

One more true sanctuary must be mentioned: St Saviour's at the end of the English Quay on the South Bank, a graceful white detail set above the dark blue water. I well remember its dedication, though the exact date escapes me: it was either 1908 or 1909. It was built in the memory of all sailors, both officers and ratings, who had perished in the Russo-Japanese war of 1904–1905. Five men of my name went down in the fatal Tzushima battle, and my grandmother left her home in Finland to be present at the dedication and to do honour to her two sons and three grandsons.

I remember an exquisite mosaic of Christ walking upon the waters of Galilee. The walls were covered with names, not a single rating forgotten, all alike from an admiral to a ship's cook, chiselled in gold.

It was indeed a fitting memorial to be built in a city of many waters and that at a place where the Moyka ran into the Neva.

Whenever I went there, I had a feeling that I was boarding a ship bound for Palestine.

★

Yet, even in spite of St Andrew's Cathedral and the cell of the Kiev Abbey, St Petersburg could not be said to share very deeply in the piety of ancient Russia. For one thing, there were so many foreigners with their own places of worship. The Holy Synod (the highest administrative body of sanctified bureaucracy) did not interfere with them so long as they abstained from propaganda.

Again, by the time I had reached my early teens, a generation was growing up to whom church going meant little more than a duty. Elderly people of all social layers, merchants and common folk (*prostoy narod*) certainly did not share that indifference, but the masses of university students and factory hands would not have cared much if all the churches in the city were to perish overnight. The great crowd of civil servants conformed most assiduously, the majority with an eye to promotion up the bureaucratic ladder. To miss a Te Deum bespoken by a superior meant a black mark in the case of a junior. 'Promote so-and-so? Well, I am not sure. He is not quite reliable, is he? He never turned up at the Te Deum on my feast day!' Not to appear at the requiem sung for a superior was an even greater crime. 'Easter duties', i.e. confession and communion, were denied their spiritual significance because they were compulsory for all the orthodox servants of the state who were obliged to bring a certificate, signed by their parish priest, to their offices.

I well remember the case of a young copying clerk at one of the ministries whose wife very nearly wrecked his career by saying in the presence of others:

'I prefer saying my prayers under God's open sky to any church going,' and she added that the North Bank of the Neva always gave her a sense of devotion that she had never experienced at a religious service.

*

None the less, if the old Muscovite piety could not be found in St Petersburg she possessed one of her very own. I can explain it in no other way than by saying that the city provided many evidences of God's existence and of His care which stood far above man-made tumults and nature-shaped savagery. In my early teens I came to learn that it was impossible to live there without some such faith, no matter what expression it took. The obscure little chapels breathed of it. The high winds sweeping from the Gulf of Finland confirmed it even when the anger of the waters broke over the islands. In the rustle of fallen leaves its whispers could be heard.

Finally, as will be told below, the sense of a great tumult to come was seldom absent from St Petersburg through all my childhood. Even through the apparently peaceful 'spells', it remained, a savagely beautiful challenge which to accept meant a confirmation of the faith. To deny it stood for a shoddy endorsement of smallness paid by the loss of integrity.

CHAPTER ELEVEN

Songs of the Four Seasons

EACH OF them was enchanting in its own way. Spring brought
one excitement after another. The first was a terrific roar as
though several artillery batteries were being discharged up and
down the river. 'The ice is about to break up', people said to
one another, and it was an unforgettable sight. On a sunny day
it was grand to watch huge blocks of ice being upended, some
among them from fifteen to twenty feet high, the sun turning
them pale green, turquoise and roseate-gold. Of all sizes and
of most fantastic shapes, those blocks made you think of a giant
jeweller's counter. The sun was not yet strong enough to melt
the ice but, once broken up, it began moving downstream

and soon rills of clear dark water could be seen here and there.

An old northern legend called it 'the giant's dawn'. The giant, never mentioned by name, was supposed to spend the winter fast asleep under the ice until the first whisper of spring reached him, and he woke up in a fury, to realize that his sanctuary was being destroyed.

Day by day it grew warmer, and yard porters were kept busy sweeping dirty green-yellow slush into the gutters. My daily walks were then somewhat restricted because so many of the lesser bridges were winched up to escape the possible damage from the up-ended ice blocks. Yet Roumiantzev Garden on Vassily Island remained easily accessible. Each day the snow under the trees went thinner and greyer until I could see blades of brave young grass pushing up here and there; the black larches became tinged with gold, and shy tiny buds appeared on the lilacs. Once sparrows took to chirping the double frames of the windows were taken out and the windows opened to let in the air, the voices in the street, the clang of wheels upon the cobbles, and the bells from a neighbouring church.

Spring was there, the cumbersome wintry clothes were being put away. Up and down the entire length of the Horse Guards Boulevard on the South Side carpenters began putting up innumerable wooden stalls for the great *Verba*, i.e. 'Pussy Willow Fair', which lasted from Palm Sunday till the following Saturday; a fair where people bought the traditional Easter presents —gaily coloured wooden eggs, beautifully carved boxes of rare Caucasian wood, hand-made lace from Valdai, richly spiced gingerbread from Viazma, and even copper samovars from Tula.

In Alexander Gardens spring marched on with first snowdrops embroidering the young grass and lilac buds opening one by one. Finally, the last ice massifs on the Neva, their earlier majesty in sad greyish tatters, moved westwards, ever faster and faster, to vanish in the sea. Soft spring winds caressed the young greenery in every street, the little bridges were back where they belonged, and peasant women from the suburbs came out with their baskets and pushcarts full of fish, eggs,

The Summer Gardens

cheese and clumsily-tied bunches of snowdrops. It was pleasant to remember that St Petersburg had been born in May.

But by the end of May many of those fragrant delights were gone, and the city entered the summer, thick leafage growing dustier and dustier from week to week. There were heat-waves when an ice-cream horn melted as soon as it was bought and when flower-beds took little, if any, refreshment from the daily application of water-cans, and thin yellow dust lay all over the pavements.

Every heat-wave usually ended in some epidemic or other—particularly cholera. Salads were forbidden; raw fruit might not be eaten with impunity, and all drinking water must be boiled. Fishmongers must have had a thin time of it through those months because fish was considered to be even more dangerous than raw fruit. We heard horrible stories of people struck by cholera after eating a supper of fried herrings and water melon.

Yet, epidemics and all, a heat-wave would break in the terrifying splendour of thunderstorms and most refreshing rain. Sometimes even the narrow Swan Stream would overflow into the Summer Gardens.

Affluent people rarely spent a summer in St Petersburg. They went abroad, or to their estates in the depths of the country, or else to fashionable resorts on the Baltic and Finnish coasts. Those less blessed by circumstance would rent a wooden *datcha*, sometimes about as comfortable as a peasant hut, in the suburbs lying to the north of the city such as Pargolovo and Oudelnayo.

We stayed where we were—except for very infrequent visits to my grandmother in the heart of Finland. Still more infrequently my Aunt Catherine would be moved to make a surprisingly kindly gesture and invite us for a week or so to her summer home in the country to the north-west of St Petersburg.

I did not mind staying in the city, but I greatly disliked the beginning of every summer.

St Petersburg had no nights between the middle of May and late June. For six weeks in the year, the strange silver light grew rather dim for about half-an-hour between sunset and dawn, but no darkness fell upon the city, and it was hard on a child to be sent to bed in strict accord with a clock's movement. At that time, as I knew, grown-up people supped after midnight, danced, read, wrote and walked into the small hours. The poets grew lyrical over 'the enchantment of St Petersburg's white nights', but I refused to share in the enthusiasm. I would lie in bed and sleep remained teasingly remote. From the wide open window, the notes of a street orchestra came into the room: the tread of many feet on the cobbles, loud talking, louder laughter and singing.

But even if the street had been quiet, there was no refreshment in 'a white night'. Somehow that strange silveriness seemed a prison. Out of its weirdness crept many an image born of unruly fantasy. The walls of the room seemed peopled by moving shapes now coming nearer, now receding, and I remember drawing the sheet over my face.

For about two or three years, between 1907 and 1910 we had a small flat on the top of a house in 12th Line on Vassily Island, and there was a most garrulous yard porter. From him I heard about any white night being a witches' festival.

He told me he had once gone to the Smolensky Cemetery at the end of the 16th Line, passed the gates, and at once turned back, shaking from head to foot.

'Why?' I asked, and the man answered in a studiedly lowered voice:

'Because all the gravestones were standing topsy-turvy and witches were dancing over them.'

I did not quite believe that tombstones could ever be turned upside down, but his mention of witches made me shudder. I had heard too much about them to deny their existence, and at once I wanted to know what they wore.

'How could I tell you, Miss? I turned back at once.'

'Then you could not have seen them—' I insisted. 'They should have been all in white or in grey, riding on broomsticks, with snakes coiled in their hair—'

The bearded man smiled a little contemptuously, but I went on:

'And sometimes they stop flying and come down to earth, waving their broomsticks right and left, and if one of their snakes as much as looks at you, you may be turned into a toad or a stone—'

He shook his head.

'Ah, that is a tale you must have read in one of your books, Miss. I have never heard folk talk about any snakes, but if a witch were to look at you, you would not be turned into anything. Her eyes would burn you as though they were lightning, and you would become a small heap of ashes, and that is no story, Miss. It happened to an uncle of mine near Tver who was a bell-ringer and always held that witches and suchlike did not exist. Well, he met one face to face, and that happened to him.'

'Did you see it?' I demanded.

'No, but my aunt came on the ashes not too far from their hut and she guessed, and my uncle was never seen again by a living soul.'

Our cook, returning from the market, overhead this remarkable dialogue, told my mother about it, and the yard porter's weird stories were ended so far as I was concerned. Yet the witches continued peopling the white nights for me. I could all too easily imagine their broomsticks and the gold green glitter of snakes in their hair. The ancient legends came into their own during those six weeks in the year, and I was thankful to see July with lush peonies sporting their pink, crimson and white in the formal beds of the Summer Gardens, with the dark falling after a tremendously colourful sunset, and the great city settling down to a night's peace unbroken by the least intrusion of unhallowed visitors.

It was good to wait for the coming of autumn when the

winds freshened and every pleasance in the city clothed itself in deep yellow, gold and bronze. A sunset would streak the Neva with fugitive flashes of gold, red and emerald green, and the islands began getting ready for the long winter. In any back yard the *droshky* men could be seen busily getting their sledges ready, oiling the iron runners, and packing hay for their passengers' feet to rest upon. Our cook went to market and brought back an armful of fragrant moss to fill in the space between the two window frames.

Daylight hours were getting shorter and shorter, and the Summer Gardens became accessible in the mornings only. The cheaper shoe-shops were crammed with brown *valenki*, boots reaching up to the knee, made of rough, thick woollen stuff—first boiled and then treated with oil to make it warm and snow-proof. The more expensive shops sold *botiky*, boots just covering the ankle, made of variedly coloured felt or velvet and thickly soled with rubber. As the days got colder, barrow-men in the streets set up their iron braziers fed with small logs. Bigger braziers were set up here and there in every market, and the house yards looked smaller and smaller for the mountains of logs stacked all over the place.

In all parks and gardens roses and other plants vanished from sight under their winter shelter of plaited twigs and thickly-packed moss. All the marble statues in the Summer Gardens and some other monuments disappeared under clumsy wooden pyramids. On Vassily Island, the waterfront grew quiet, the last steamers having made for the open sea.

Soon the first snow of the year began powdering the pavements. That first snowfall always reminded me of ballet dancing. The flakes, obedient to every breath of the wind, moved so gracefully. They did not fall: rather, they descended, the intricate and miraculous pattern of each flake a joy to look at. Then the wind roughened, the snow came down thicker and

faster and St Isaac's Cathedral, for one, looked like a gigantic
strawberry lavishingly dusted with rough sugar. Little by little
the snow stopped melting on the dark-blue breast of the Neva
and hardened into chips of thin ice which grew in size and
thickness day by day, until by mid November the ice was
declared safe, and wooden foot-bridges were thrown from one
bank to another. Men, shod in *valenki* and smothered in sheep-
skins, began building snow mountains in every public park and
garden. Those delights were free to all children who possessed
a sled, though we had to pay a few coppers for keeping our
sleds in a wooden lean-to at the back of the snow-mountain.

It was a busy time for the municipality. Blizzards came early
enough; sometimes they lasted for hours and left gigantic
drifts in their wake. Men, armed with brooms and spades would
clear both pavements and roads, packing the snow into tidy,
low walls, with an opening every few yards. A little later came
great lorries and the snow walls would come down, be loaded
on to the lorries and taken away.

The marine police kept a watchful eye on the Neva even
when the ice seemed solid enough. They would stick poles,
topped with a red flag, wherever they thought the ice was unsafe.
Yet those experts were not infallible. On New Year's day in
1909 my mother and I were coming home from Alexander
Gardens. As usual, she chose to cross the river by the wooden
foot-bridge and I made for a path curving across at some
distance from the bridge. I could not see a single pole with the
red flag anywhere.

I was running on the hard-beaten snow when, a few dozen
yards away from Nicholas Quay, I felt my feet slipping and
my whole body going down and down. I don't remember
hearing screams from the foot-bridge. I don't really remember
anything until I knew that my hands were clawing at someone's
beard and that I was being carried to the safety of the quay. It

was a marine policeman. I also remember my mother running up and the man whistling for a *droshky*. When we got home, all my clothes had to be cut off me—they were just ice. I was at once put into a warm bed, but I did not even get a cold in the head.

Later, I learned that I had fallen into what they called 'a black water patch' with thin ice on top, some five or six feet of water underneath and the solid ice below. If the man had not rescued me I would have been sucked away.

My mother, having a single twenty copek coin in her purse, had given her card to the man and asked him to call. But he never came. Instead, two important officials visited the flat, expressed their horror and sympathy, and reimbursed my mother for the *droshky* and all my ruined clothes.

That experience, however, did not rob me of my love for the Neva.

★

The focal point of any winter was Christmas. Our English relations and friends sometimes did not remember that Russia still followed the old style and was thirteen days behind the West. Some exciting parcels from England and from my mother's sisters in Rome often arrived at the end of November. I would be allowed to cut out the stamps and no more: the contents were put away till Christmas morning.

It was possible, as it were, 'to smell' Christmas near every market where beautifully-shaped firs of many sizes turned the spaces between the stalls into something like an entrance to a magic forest. Even when snow fell on them, it looked silver and every delicate frond gained in beauty. Our own tree came from St Andrew's Market, and the choosing of it was quite an occasion. My mother, our cook and I went together immediately after the noon meal, the cook clutching a measuring tape in her thickly gauntleted hand. It wanted but two days till Christmas, and St Andrew's was all hard-beaten snow underfoot, metallic breaths of frosty air, shopping crowds, shouting pedlars, and trees without number. But the crowds were good-humoured, the pedlars grinned, the stallholders, laughing and sometimes swearing in broken Russian, Finnish and German, belonged to the hour and the mood.

We always went to the same stall where the man knew us well, and my own choice would fall on a tree which could never have got inside the flat. My mother would shake her head, the cook smiled, stretched out the tape, looked at it for a moment, then raised her shawled head and pointed at a tree.

'But you have not measured it—' cried my mother.

'That I have, *Baryna*,' said the cook, 'my eyes have told me.'

She was never proved wrong.

There followed the usual business of fixing the price; the portly stallholder, in between weighing out nuts and caramels, found time to engage our sympathy, his wife being laid up with some mysterious ailment. Then an errand boy would be whistled for and the tree swung over his shoulder.

We tramped back to the flat in the swiftly gathering shadows. The brief winter day was over, street lamps began glittering here and there but, on reaching the quay, the majesty of the frosty dark enclosed us wholly. For a reason I can't remember, the waterfront lights were the very last to be lit. There was scarcely any traffic, and within the strange and lovely silence we moved on until the errand-boy, shifting the tree from one shoulder to another, broke into an old Finnish song about the spirit living in the tiniest snowflake. The tune was slow, and the unfamiliar words deepened the mystery all around us.

On reaching our house, the boy would stagger up the stairs, lean the tree against the door, and wait for his reward—a couple of apples and a copper.

On Christmas Eve we decorated the tree with round-shaped white and pink gingerbread, each piece having a hole in the middle for the string to get through, some tiny tablets of chocolate in red, green and purple foil, a dozen or so of small red-cheeked apples and gilt walnuts. The other decorations, bought at Peto's, were kept from one year to another—tiny sedan chairs, violins, bears, monkeys and fishes in silver foil and in gold, minute tin candlesticks tulip-shaped and painted all the colours of the rainbow, and a gilt star for the top. All in all, there was no grandeur. In those days you could not buy gay wrapping paper, and the few gifts lay on the floor with no secrecy—just two or three of them: a box of pens and pencils, a few Tauchnitz volumes, and always a stout copybook for my 'scribbling'.

The oil lamp would be put out—the little candles were lit, the room felt warm, the splendour of winter lay over St Petersburg, and it was Christmas Day. What more could a child ask for?

The Admiralty
and
St Isaac's Cathedral

CHAPTER TWELVE

Occasions Great and Small

THE CITY was not really very large as capitals go. Yet, with a
wide river, vast squares and broad avenues, it was impossible
to escape the sense of space in St Petersburg. None the less,
when, about 1905 or 1906, they started building an immense

rotunda at the back of the Zoological Museum and people learned that it would house a mammoth found in a perfect condition in a deep ravine in Eastern Siberia, everybody got excited. There were pictures in the papers. Lectures were given in public halls, and talks in all the schools. Curiosity reached its peak when we heard that it was coming to St Petersburg, but we had to wait quite a time before the rotunda was open to the public.

The mammoth was put behind a wall of thick glass, his position just as it had been for more than a million years—crouching on his hind legs, the enormous head thrust forward, the terrible tusks as menacing as they must have been before history began. He crouched there, surrounded by huge blocks of ice, and he looked terribly alive. Children had heard so much about him and seen so many pictures; his coming across Siberia and Central Russia must have meant a miracle of haulage, and the work done upon him in St Petersburg—a triumph for learned zoologists and many others. But the reality surpassed everything. Wisely enough, the Museum authorities would not allow children to go in unless they were accompanied by adults. From the great doorway the wall of glass did not seem to be there at all, and the first impression I got was that of a monster about to pounce and leap across. I felt as cold as though I were plunged into a deep tub of ice, closed my eyes, and clutched a stranger's hand, forgetting that my mother was close to me. But, during the next visit, the fear got less and less until it became possible to walk right up to the glass wall and to look without shuddering.

No sooner did St Petersburg get more or less accustomed to that marvel than another monstrous visitor arrived, this time by water, and was moored alongside the English Quay on the South Bank. I think he came at the end of the summer of 1907. He was a huge whale caught and killed not far from Archangel in the White Sea. He was most interesting but he did not inspire terror. Experts had so worked on him that it was possible to get inside and walk up and down on wooden planks which stretched from his tail to his head. Oil lamps swung to and fro overhead, and it was so warm that a boy said loudly:

'Well, Jonah must have been quite comfortable inside *his* whale!'

The monster, if I remember rightly, was well over one hundred feet long. For all the work done on him, there remained a very powerful odour, and few were the people who lingered inside. They preferred scrambling onto the quay and staring at the great head with its curiously small eyes. A docker was heard saying:

'That creature could overturn a big boat as easily as you peel a potato!'

When summer slipped into autumn, the visitor was tugged away towards the sea. He did not return to St Petersburg.

The most momentous annual occasion was the New Year's day. Florists were said to make fortunes from hothouse lilac, mimosa and lilies. The traditional greeting would be heard at every corner: 'New Year, new happiness' ('*S novym godom, s novym stchastiem*'), and the social pivot of it all was the great reception at the Winter Palace.

The Emperor and his family would leave Tsarskoe Selo for the capital. All the members of the dynasty, the diplomatic corps, the Government and senior civil servants together with many generals and admirals attended a solemn Te Deum in the palace chapel. The service over, the reception would be held in one of the great halls, all the women wearing the traditional Russian dress, a *kokshnik* on the head and a wide-sleeved *sarafan* over a brocade kirtle.

Now in the early autumn of 1907, by a mere chance I made friends with the two children of the Siamese minister. It happened in the Summer Gardens. I believe it had something to do with a big multicoloured ball thrown by the little girl so high that it got stuck on a forked limb of a lime tree—some ten or fifteen feet from the ground. No keeper was in sight and the boy, younger than his sister, obviously could not climb. It meant no effort for me to retrieve the ball, and the two children at once carried me off to meet their very prim, rather elderly English governess, and later their parents met my mother. Our own circumstances, of course, did not permit of any intimate contacts with the Legation world but the children and I continued meeting and playing in the Summer Gardens. In the end I was invited to join the brother and sister together with Miss Jackson just outside the Winter Palace entrance where the general public could not get in.

We stood on the well-beaten snow for quite a time before the first carriage arrived. I held my breath. It was the New Year's day, and exciting things were bound to happen.

They did. The coachman reined in, a footman jumped down from the box, the carriage door was flung open, and for the first time I saw a Grand-Duchess in full court dress, the em-pearled *kokoshnik* on her head, a silver brocade *sarafan* glittering with jewels, a magnificent brocade kirtle, and the broad red ribbon of St Catherine's Order across her breast. The day was bitterly cold, but she wore her sable cloak so casually that it hid none of the splendours. Her feet shod in thin silver slippers, she did not hurry past, and the smile she gave us was enchanting. Miss Jackson dropped a perfect curtsey and I, however clumsily, followed her example.

When all the splendours had vanished, the little Siamese boy whispered in English:

'Was she one of the Emperor's daughters?'

'Oh no—' I whispered back, 'his daughters are all in the palace already and they are much younger.'

Later I learned that she was Grand-Duchess Helen, daughter

of Grand-Duke Wladimir, and mother of Marina, the late dowager Duchess of Kent.

We stood where we were, but so many carriages came up that we lost count of them, and at last Miss Jackson decided it was time to leave. We all but ran across the vast Palace Square, through the great archway of the General Staff Headquarters, on to Morskaya Street where the two little Siamese stopped at Berrin's door. Obviously, Miss Jackson had received very particular instructions. It was New Year's day with gaiety and a touch of madness in the air, and the four of us sat down at a round mahogany table, drank piping hot chocolate and fortified ourselves with sponge fingers and éclairs.

We had eaten and drunk when we saw two little girls' faces pressed against the nearest window. Their coats were even shabbier than mine and I was wishing I were hostess with money in my pockets, when the two Siamese scrambled down, the boy seizing a plateful of sponge fingers and his sister another of éclairs.

'What are you doing?' cried the governess, but they were by the door, the boy saying over his shoulder that it was New Year's day, and his sister piping rather impertinently:

'This is St Petersburg and not London, Miss Jackson.'

The cakes and the plates were given to the little girls, the boy and his sister came back, flushed with their triumph, and the unfortunate governess, having first fumbled in her purse, had to explain to the waiter whose children they were, and that the bill was to be sent to the Siamese Legation.

Those Siamese soon vanished from my landscape, their father being appointed either to Paris or Washington but, their very names long since gone from memory, I have never forgotten that New Year's day of 1908—not so much because of the blinding splendours seen at the Palace entrance, but because a little Siamese girl had said 'This is St Petersburg', as though, all unconsciously, she had gathered up some of its magic into her innermost thoughts. The city was beautifully cosmopolitan and unusual but, primarily, it was itself, a place where just anything could happen, where nothing stood still, where sharp social contrasts all but met face to face, where the backyard of a great mansion looked on a lane as slummy as any in Europe, where you could be shabby and too poor to afford jam for your tea and yet keep the sense of race inviolate, where you could talk to dockers and humble shopkeepers and never be conscious of the difference in accent and manner. That—across the years —still seems a part of St Petersburg's magic.

Yet another annual moment of importance broke out on Palm Sunday when the great fair was opened on the Horse Guards Boulevard which stretched from St Isaac's Cathedral to Annunciation Square, a distance not much under a mile. The fair was commonly known as *Verba*, i.e. pussy-willow— since branches of this decorated homes and churches. *Verba* lasted a whole week—from Palm Sunday until the next Saturday. The entire length of the wide boulevard was crowded with stalls. In between, pedlars hawked oddly coloured sweets, paper wind-mills, crudely painted wooden crocodiles, hot apples studded with cloves and poppy seeds, and multicoloured balloons.

The stalls sold superior wares, beautifully carved boxes of chestnut and lime wood, lengths of hand-made lace from Valdai, candied fruits from the Crimea and the Caucasus, necklaces of porcelain, glass and semi-precious stones, caviar from Astrakhan, gingerbread from Tula and Wiazma in elegant pink boxes, cunningly carved napkin rings, and much else. But Easter eggs stood in the foreground.

Farmers' wives from the Baltic provinces sold real hen's eggs in round baskets cushioned with green and grey moss, a fluffy chick artlessly made of pale yellow wool in the middle.

But such eggs were 'ordinary', and few people bought them. There were terribly expensive eggs made of white china with views of St Petersburg painted on them; eggs of clear glass with the Resurrection scene inside; eggs of fragrant soap dyed green and yellow; wooden eggs of all sizes and colours. Finally, a few stalls, more solidly timbered than the others, exhibited tiny eggs of jasper, malachite, porphyry, amethyst, silver, gold and rock crystal. Some were laid on squares of rather dusty black velvet. Others were housed in tiny cardboard boxes. One stall, usually presided over by a fierce-looking Circassian, sold nothing but necklaces of tiny silver eggs.

The crowds were so thick that it took more than two hours to get to the end of the boulevard. The noise was deafening. Here and there you came on a stall selling refreshments—hot milk in thick white mugs, currant buns, chunks of highly peppered *kolbassa* (salami), pickled herrings and lemons, slabs of walnut cheese (*halva*), and generous slices of bread commonly called *sitny*.

I think that *Verba* was the one occasion in the year when St Petersburg tried to be Russian; when it disowned, as it were, its alien beginnings, and drowned itself in an unbuttoned Russian zest for pleasure. For one week in the year, Peter the Great's city seemed to recognize its allegiance to a past where St Petersburg was nothing and Moscow was all.

My mother and I went there in the middle of the week— mainly to purchase Easter eggs, but the crowds were so dense, the noise so overpowering that I cannot remember a single occasion when I made a satisfying purchase. Ah yes! There was one. At the very end of the boulevard, close to Annunciation Square, stood a ramshackle little stall, and the old woman in a vast blue apron sold nothing but wooden fruit. There I bought a crudely painted apple and a rather fantastic pear. My mother said:

'I thought you were going to buy Easter eggs—'

'I have bought them,' I replied.

But *Verba* lasted just one week, and the city had to wait till Trinity Sunday for another great moment of the year. It was a fragrant green moment when the shops and houses, to say nothing of churches, were festooned and garlanded with green branches of birch. All the carriages, horse-buses and even little boats on the river carried them. The fine texture of the leaves gleamed in the sun. All through the long day the city was one great swathe of green. Towards evening the branches would wilt and their leafage turn yellow. By Monday morning they were gone. I believe the custom was Slavic in origin but, whether home-born or imported, it certainly accorded well with the city's landscape.

Those were annual occasions. Yet there were others which came and struck a myriad lights from the background of ordinary days. One such happened in February 1913, a great year for Russia in that it marked the tercentenary of the Romanov dynasty. Preparations had begun some two or three years before. Particularly beautiful postage stamps were designed and put into circulation; finely enamelled cups, mugs and plates with the portraits of Nicholas II and Michael, the first Romanov (1613–1645), were seen in jewellers' windows, and even second-rate drapers exhibited rather gaudy scarves and handkerchiefs with crude portraits of Nicholas and Michael stamped in the middle.

St Petersburg, a Romanov creation, went all out to celebrate with flags and huge tinsel crowns on every public building; the municipality and wealthy merchants voted enormous sums for gifts and meals in all the free schools, almshouses, and hospitals. Beggars were not forgotten. No money was to be given them but a large bundle of warm clothing and a meal of a kind none of them had ever dreamt about.

The great day in February started with all the bells ringing and military bands playing all over the city. The focal point was the Kazan Cathedral where the Metropolitan of St Petersburg was to officiate at a solemn Te Deum and massed cathedral choirs sing the appointed litanies. Crowds began converging on Nevsky Prospect long before dawn. Some hours before the Imperial carriage was to appear, not an inch of space was left between Nevsky and the Winter Palace. My Aunt Fanny's dressmaker had her workshop on the second floor of a house opposite the Cathedral, and my mother and I were offered the hospitality of a window. Thus I was lucky enough to observe a scene never to be forgotten down the years.

A great open sledge drawn by four greys and surrounded by a troop of mounted cossacks all in brown and silver, drove very slowly round the curve of the Kazan Gardens. But neither the cossacks nor the police were needed that day.

From where we watched it seemed as though the whole population of St Petersburg had come out to mob the Imperial carriage. As it drew up by the steps leading up to the Cathedral porch, the shy wintry sun came out and sharpened the splendour. The deafening hurrahs drowned all other sounds as the Emperor, his wife and daughters began ascending the steps. Outside, the crowds were waiting for the service.

We moved away from our window and accepted cups of most welcome coffee. The dressmaker, a plump, untidy woman in a black dress and a blonde wig ran about with a plate of biscuits, exclaiming every other minute: 'What a day! What a star of a day!'

There were about ten people in the room, all strangers to us, among them a tall thin girl most elegantly dressed in velvet and furs. When the little dressmaker came out yet again with her 'what a star of a day!' the girl put down her empty cup, gathered up her muff, and made for the door, remarking over her shoulder:

The Emperor Nicholas II

Winter Palace

'I should call it a falling star!'

For a moment nobody spoke. Then an elderly naval officer sighed, and the dressmaker took to wringing her hands.

'Would you have believed it? A falling star indeed! And that from a countess!' she added. 'Daughter of a customer, too!'

An awkward silence followed until someone came out with a platitude about young people carried away by any nonsense they heard.

I think we all forgot the remark about 'the falling star' when the Cathedral bells sent us back to the windows. Presently the Emperor's great sledge started on its return journey to the Winter Palace, and once again the cossack escort had to draw back because of men, women and children shouting 'hurrahs', clapping and singing.

When daylight went, St Petersburg blazed with the glory of most intricate illuminations. The entire waterfront, both on the North and South Sides, was drowned in colour. Here and there, in between crowns and sceptres, appeared the gigantic words of the first line of the National Anthem 'God save the Tzar' (*Bozhe Tzaria Khrani*) picked out in violet and green, in crimson and gold. The front of the great building of the Academy of Sciences founded by Catherine I, Peter the Great's second wife, blazed with an enormous transparency showing the Founder of St Petersburg in workman's clothes, a peasant cap on his head and a hammer in his hands.

Even the humble Roumiantzev Garden shared in the splendour, multicoloured lamps, shaped like crowns, swinging from tree to tree. Nicholas Bridge burned crimson and violet from end to end, and Konradi's, a sweet shop facing the bridge, distributed tiny chocolate medallions, '1613–1913' stamped in gold on scarlet foil, to all the children passing by.

As the evening deepened, fireworks came into play across the ice-bound Neva. All were designed to do honour to the great national moment, and the *pièce de résistance* was in the shape of the entire National Anthem, green word by green word leaping skywards. It was bitterly cold—but the crowds kept running about, stamping their feet on the hard snow, clapping their fur-gauntleted hands, and sometimes halting at a corner to drink a mug of piping hot tea, their eyes never leaving the river.

★

On July 21st of the same year, 1913, I reached my fifteenth birthday. That afternoon one of the greatest surprises broke upon me.

My father's family was very numerous and most wildly scattered all over the Empire. He had a sister much older than himself who lived, married and died in St Petersburg years before my arrival. She had an only daughter, Elizabeth, who was sixteen when I came, and very vaguely I remember her wedding to a wealthy senior civil servant who was soon appointed to the governorship of a province east of the Volga.

Elizabeth was one of the most exciting cousins I had: elegant, intelligent, beautiful, she seemed to consider life in terms of a flowered landscape. She came to St Petersburg about once every two years, never called on us, but most punctiliously invited us to a regal tea at the *Hôtel d'Europe* where she always stayed. Her clothes and her laughter were enchanting. So was her kindliness: she never forgot to push a promisingly bulky parcel into my hands when we left. Otherwise, there would come an infrequent picture postcard or two.

And that afternoon Elizabeth, in shimmering blue silk and a flowery cartwheel of a hat, appeared in her carriage at the yard gates of the house on the 9th Line of Vassily Island where my mother and I lived in one room on the top floor of an enormous tenement. The yard porter, struck dumb by the appearance of a private carriage, swung open the double gates, and Elizabeth leant forward and asked where exactly did 'her Excellency' live?'

My father had died the year before; he had been a professor of chemistry but, according to the prevailing law, he had also held a civil rank and died as 'a Real State Councillor' (*deysvitelniy statskiy sovietnik*) which entitled my mother to the most inconvenient honour of 'her Excellency', which she used as seldom as she could. Certainly, the yard porter at No 44 never imagined that a civil general's widow could possibly live in rooms, but he pointed the little entrance to the coachman and, as Elizabeth told us later, remained in the middle of the yard, bowing from his hips every now and then.

'Just as if he were wound up like a clock,' she said.

She mounted right up to the sixth floor, knocked at the door, and burst in, all silk and scent and smiles.

'I came to St Petersburg two days ago, and yesterday had tea at Aunt Catherine's, and Natalie mentioned a birthday. So I have come to take Poppy for a drive and get her a little present. Is that all right, Aunt Olga? Oh, what a view you have! Why, surely, it is the sea just beyond, isn't it?'

She chattered, and I slipped behind the screen in a corner to change into the only finery I possessed: a white muslin blouse and a blue linen skirt. My hat was a modest straw affair, trimmed with bits of blue ribbon and bought at a cheap shop on Vassily Island. It was the case of a sparrow and a bird of paradise, but Elizabeth was too well bred to make comment either on my clothes or on the other evidences of our poverty, and went on singing praises of the view and inviting us both to a meal at the end of the week.

As we drove across the great yard, the burly porter still standing and bowing, she asked me what I would like to have.

'Oh, a book, please,' I mumbled, and Elizabeth told the coachman to drive to Watkins'.

I gasped and became tongue-tied. Watkins', the English bookshop, was in Morskaya Street just off Nevsky Prospect. Often enough I had passed its windows but never been inside. Watkins' sold no second-hand books, and its riches were about as accessible as the top of Mount Everest. Now I heard that I was to choose as many books as I liked.

'My man will take them up those stairs for you,' went on Elizabeth. 'I must get back to my hotel but the carriage will return and you need not hurry.' She added casually: 'Please mention my name. I have an account there.'

After something like a half-hour of amazement, delight and anguish I chose *The Vicar of Wakefield*, *Les Misérables*, an illustrated German biography of Peter the Great, Feuillet's *Histoire de la Philosophie*, *The Voyage of the Beagle* and, as a light-weight, a novel by Marie Corelli. Then I stopped, suddenly and shamefully conscious of having been greedy, but the huge parcel was being wrapped up and Elizabeth's carriage was already outside. The elderly coachman, his mistresse's absence loosening his tongue, became most talkative as the beautifully groomed chestnuts turned into Horseguards Boulevard.

'See, Miss, I am a countryman, born and bred at Uzhinky in the Tver Province, but the mistress was born here, and she loves St Petersburg so, but how can she come often—all the long, long way, from across the Volga? His Excellency's province is not round the corner as the saying goes—'

He went on and on in a peasant's comfortably drowsy voice, but we had already crossed Nicholas Bridge and I am afraid I gave up listening. It was good to know that Elizabeth loved the city. Somehow that turned the day into a phrase of music.

My mother and I lunched with her later on, she brushing away my rather incoherent thanks. Not one of us three knew that we would never meet again; 1914 brought the war, and Elizabeth gave herself up to the Red Cross activities in her husband's vast province. There were a few postcards and no more, and the vortex of 1917 put a stop to all communication, but the memory of her still remains: so much at home with her own kind and with peasants, always gay and grateful for everything life gave to her, a charming hostess and, for all her infrequent visits to the north, a most affectionate cousin. When I think of her now, I remember her coachman's words. St Petersburg had moulded her earliest years, and in the memory the city and she stand together.

*

A little more than a year later Russia was at war with Germany. According to ancient custom the Emperor was to read the manifesto first in St Petersburg and then in Moscow. It fell on a fearfully hot July day in 1914; I trudged along the University Quay and caught glimpses of crowds milling along Palace Bridge. I had heard that the Emperor and his wife were to appear on the balcony facing the vast Palace Square, and rather foolishly I hoped to find my way to it, but when I got to the bridge, my heart sank: there was no room for a pin to fall.

Suddenly I heard hoofbeats behind me and, turning, saw my cousin Alexander, head of the family, mounted on a beautiful grey, a troop of men riding behind. He was years older than me and we met very seldom, but he recognized me, reined in, and, leaning down from the saddle, asked what I was doing there. Cheeks crimson, I explained. He whistled and turned to a man behind him.

'Mount the young lady and take her to the side entrance of the General Staff Headquarters.' Here he turned to another: 'You ride ahead and tell them, and I will see to the rest.'

So I rode pillion across the bridge, past the high railings of the Winter Palace, and across the vast square. The man reined in at a very small door of the General Staff Headquarters. A sergeant on duty came out and led me up a narrow stair to a wide red-carpeted passage. At a door a young man in the Hussar uniform seemed to be waiting for me. All in a daze I entered a big panelled room, its three windows facing the Palace Square. The officer pushed an armchair towards one of them, handed me a pair of field-glasses and said almost apologetically:

'The General thought you would get a good view from here, but I am afraid it will take some time before their Majesties come out. There is a Te Deum and all at the Palace. Have you had lunch?'

I shook my head, thanked him for the loan of the field-glasses, and stared out of the window. The entire space of the square was packed tight with people. The young officer bowed and left me. Presently a batman came, carrying a laden tray. I feasted on a chicken cutlet cushioned in savoury rice, followed by lemon jelly and iced coffee. I enjoyed it all but my eyes went on wandering to the window. Hardly any room for a pin to fall there; all the men were bare-headed, and everybody's eyes were riveted on the great crimson-draped balcony of the Palace.

Presently the batman came to fetch the tray and said:

'The Te Deum is finished, Miss. Their Majesties will be out on the balcony any moment, *baryshna*.'

'Thank you—' I murmured.

Below, the crowd stirred once or twice, then grew very still. I could see the great balcony doors swing open, and the Emperor and Empress appeared. He wore the ordinary uniform of a colonel of an infantry regiment, she was all in white, a great picture hat on her small head. I saw him come to the very edge of the balcony parapet. He was speaking but I could not hear what he said.

I turned the field-glasses towards that immense crowd below, thousands and thousands of them, and then I saw them fall down on their knees. Some instinct made me push the window open, and I heard the National Anthem chanted by the crowd. The Emperor lifted his hand, and his wife bowed. The anthem finished, they vanished from the balcony and the great doors swung to, but the crowds would not disperse. One patriotic song after another followed the Anthem.

Later, having duly thanked my cousin, I slogged home on foot. The city seemed at once excited and calm, and I thought that Peter the Great, having fought and bested the Swedes, would think that a war with Germany was small beer indeed.

Taurida Palace

CHAPTER THIRTEEN

Waves of Tumults

IN A SENSE, nobody could live in St Petersburg, and that some decades before I was born, without a consciousness of volcanic anger 'just round the corner', about to erupt. Nobody quite knew how or when it would happen.

Now, my family on both sides was never directly concerned with political issues. They were all absorbed in literature, science and arts. Naturally they could not help being aware of the unease which, from the very beginning of this century, reached the level of violent action in terms of murders, strikes, mutinies among the peasants and in the services, and frequently brutal reprisals carried out by the authorities.

In 1904 I was six; I knew nothing of those larger issues, but I

knew already that there were many dark corners in the city and
that there existed penury which made our own poverty seem
wealth by comparison. There were a great many things we could
not afford but, at least, we lived in decent flats and later in rooms.
It was from my mother's maids that I learned about people
who could not manage the rent of a single room, lived in
damp corners, and considered themselves lucky to have even a
leaking roof over their heads; people who fed once a day on
rough rye bread and thin cabbage soup, and tried to forget
their hunger by nightfall when they huddled under worn-out
blankets and even horse-cloths on their pallets. I listened to
those stories most painfully, and considered such folk as 'the
honest poor'—unlike many whimpering beggars under church
porches and street corners.

But it was not poverty alone that went to the shaping of the
tumults in my childhood. It was something else. I could not
give it a name and it seemed all the more threatening. I can
illustrate it no better than by remembering my confusion and
anger when, at the end of 1904, I first read a big notice at the
gates of the Summer Gardens.

'Dogs, beggars, all lower ranks (*nizhnye chiny*) of the Army
and the Navy not allowed inside.'

I read it slowly, but I could not understand how such a
notice came to be put up. I asked my nurse. She merely
shrugged.

'I can't read—' she mumbled, 'you read it aloud, *Baryshna*.'

I did and said angrily:

'Dogs can't read either or beggars. And why should soldiers
and sailors be kept out?'

The nurse pursed her lips and glanced behind. Much later I
realized that she feared a policeman would overhear me, but
there was not one in sight. Her reply, however, did not satisfy
me.

'It is God's will, *baryshna*, and the Tsar's. So nothing can be done about it.'

But my little mind was already plunged into confusion, and the very few people to whom I later tried to explain it, suggested that I should leave it alone.

'You are far too small to understand anything about it.'

But I was not too small for the hurt and anger that soldiers and sailors were put on the same level as dogs and beggars.

One morning at the beginning of 1905, there was nothing except porridge for breakfast, and I heard that all the bakers and milkmen were on strike.

'What is a strike?' I asked, and got no answer.

Later that day my nurse took me for a walk. We went down Nicholas Quay, passed the Academy of Arts, and were there stopped by a worried policeman.

'Take the young lady home—' he said to Anna; 'there is trouble ahead—'

The nurse tugged at my sleeve, but I shook her off. Further ahead, I could see a crowd moving towards us, red flags flapping wildly in the wind.

'There they are—' the policeman said gruffly. 'Take her home, I say.'

The crowd moved nearer, singing a song I did not recognize. Later I knew it was the *Marsellaise*. The policeman's gruffness must have frightened me. I clutched Anna's hand and we turned back.

I did not know it at the time, but it was the procession of university students on their way to join the strikers from the steel factories down the river.

That day, my mother being out, I heard a loud excited voice from the kitchen—to me a forbidden ground but, remembering the incident in the morning, I ventured greatly and opened the door an inch or two. The burly, bearded yard porter was sitting at a table, a glass of steaming tea in front of him. The cook, my nurse and the two maids leant forward, listening greedily. Nobody noticed me.

The man talked about the factory people who would soon seize the city, gatecrash into the palaces, sit on velvet chairs, and dine off salmon and pineapple. He said he had heard that many gendarmes and policemen were soon to be 'strung up on lamp-posts, and the workers come into their own'. The cook frowned, my nurse stared, and the others kept nodding their heads.

Many, if not all, of those details wholly beyond my comprehension, I was none the less frightened. I crept back to my nursery and decided that the notice seen near the gateway to the Summer Gardens was at the bottom of the business. It did not mention factory people but, for all I knew, they stood on the same level with beggars, soldiers and sailors.

For several days I had to forego my daily walk, my mother saying 'there is great trouble in the streets. Some day you'll come to understand it.'

Much was happening in the city, though I witnessed none of it. Workmen from the Gutuevsky and Putilovsky were on strike; there were barricades in the streets, and students from the University were joined by the young men from the Technological College and the Institute of Mines. Mounted police and cossacks were called out, and armed guards were sent to protect palaces and churches. Many shops—particularly on Nevsky Prospect, re-inforced their shutters by iron bars. The big yard gate into the house where we lived was bolted and barred. So was the front door, the fat *schweizar*'s (hall porter) authority re-inforced rather oddly by a frightened, seedy assistant from the nearest shoeshop.

What was happening outside? The servants, brushing aside the yard porter's protests, ventured into the streets once or twice, and came back, their imaginations on fire with all the things heard at the nearest corner.

A bank had been burned down; a troop of cossacks had scattered a students' procession on Palace Bridge, many of the young men being trampled to death; meat and flour were running short and nothing except root vegetables could be bought at St Andrew's Market. One hundred workmen from a cotton mill down the river had tried to break their way into the Winter Palace, and it was obvious that everybody in St Petersburg would either starve to death or perish from the cold.

Some of it was true, but most was imagined, and nobody, certainly not the excited servants, could or would tell me what it was all about. My mother kept me indoors, and some sixth sense urged me not to ask questions, still less to admit that I had been listening to kitchen gossip. Neither milk nor eggs appeared at breakfast. But within a few days the great yard gates were open, and they stayed open. Tradesmen trudged up the back stairs, a pair of shoes was taken away by a cobbler, and the milk jug reappeared on the table. Presently, my mother and I walked right down to the end of the University Quay. There were no processions to bar the way. I stared about but I could see neither cossacks nor mounted police. The shops between the Academy of Arts and Nicholas Bridge stood open. The pale wintry sunlight fell across the Neva, and people went about as usual, shopping, talking, laughing, grumbling. The city seemed just the same—except for a broken window pane here and there, but I felt something had happened and more— that it would happen again.

The sharp tumult of the first Revolution lay behind us, but much of its climate remained. The Winter Palace was empty, the Emperor and his family having left the capital never to live there again. Soon after we moved to the 9th Line. The house we lived in faced the Young Women's College where girls, having finished with their ordinary schooling, continued their studies since at that time they were not allowed to enter the University. A great many of them came from the country and lived in hostels. Most of them were poor; they looked shabby and grave, hurrying to lectures, batches of books under their arms. One afternoon, the street was cordoned off by police. As the girls, the last lecture over, began streaming out of the great building, they were stopped, their identity documents examined by the police, and quite a number of them were marched off, surrounded by a posse of mounted gendarmes. The last girl gone, the great doors were padlocked by a police-man. Within a few minutes the street wore its ordinary air—but some unease remained, and a fat greengrocer, putting a cabbage into a customer's basket, was heard gloomily muttering about bombs and conspirators. The word *svoboda* occurred again and again, and hearing it, I decided that 'freedom' was something not to welcome but to run away from, the kind of monster encountered in Grimm's tales. From the yard porter I learned that many among the girl-students had been mixed up in 'the Revolution'; they had marched alongside the men-students, carrying red flags and singing dangerous songs, and carrying bombs in brown paper parcels.

'All of which,' concluded the man, 'goes to prove that females had best stay illiterate. The more they read, the more rubbish they learn.'

I did not agree with him, but I was too young to start an argument.

Anna, a raw country girl, could explain nothing, and the other two maids were equally stupid. Not so, however, our cook, middle-aged, experienced, born of a poor peasant family in the Baltic Provinces and having worked in St Petersburg since her youth, Magda certainly had 'ideas', though she pre-ferred keeping most of them to herself. She left us in 1907, I think, and went back to her village in Kurland. Her successor was a plump red-cheeked Russian from Novgorod, capable enough in the kitchen but rather loquacious and overtly scornful of my mother's Russian.

'What did you say, *Baryna*? Two cats for the young *Baryshna*'s lunch? Bless us and save us! I am a Christian! I have never cooked a cat in my life, *Baryna*, and I am not going to now.'

A cat was *koshka* in Russian. The small fish my mother meant me to have were known as *koriushka*! My brother came in and interpreted and my mother left the kitchen, annoyance on her face.

But now we were still in 1905, and Magda reigned in the kitchen. By a lucky chance I found her alone making pastry.

'What was it all about?' I ventured.

'All for *svoboda* (freedom), Miss,' she replied, busily plying the rolling-pin. 'And it all came to nothing! But something is sure to happen again,' and she pursed her lips.

That marked the end of my kitchen excursions. I could not understand what *svoboda* meant, but I felt that whatever was to happen in the future would make one take no notice of empty milk-jugs and closed yard gates. Yet I was barely seven at the time. The Russo-Japanese war had ended most disastrously; the delicately enamelled Japanese trays, silk-printed fans mounted on ivory sticks, and transparently fragile china had long since vanished from the windows of Alexandre, Knopf, and other grand shops in the Mayfair of St Petersburg, and they did not appear ever again, but that was an unimportant urban detail.

From now on Tsarkoselsky Station was barred to all curious outsiders. The great space in front was girdled by policemen. There ran blood-curdling stories of bombs found on the permanent way between St Petersburg and Tsarskoe Selo, of men crouching in dark corners, loaded revolvers in their pockets, of bogus waitresses in the railway restaurant who were seen putting arsenic into salt-cellars and sugar bowls. To me, it was all hearsay, though I felt the impress of such things on days when either my mother or a maid accompanied me on my walk, or I had to stay indoors.

One wintry night in 1907 we all woke up to the loud clang of fire-engine bells. A great lending library on the 6th Line of Vassily Island was on fire. It was a windy night, and flames, having devoured one big house, now ran to the right and to the left, demolishing several shops and a few private houses. In the morning columns of acrid smoke were seen spiralling up to the pale blue wintry sky, and firemen were still at work. Every fire station in St Petersburg had sent its men to fight the fire. I went with our Russian cook to St Andrew's Market. On the steps of St Andrew's Cathedral, a middle-aged man in a shabby civil service uniform was saying that the fire had been a piece of incendiarism.

'Looks like it—' muttered our cook and hurried me on.

The market was full of it. Some blamed the 'revolutionaries', others—the police for not having prevented it in time; still others alleged that for many days past 'mysterious' figures could be seen slipping down into the library basement. 'It was petrol and oil they were taking, I wager—' said a butcher, wrapping up some pork chops for our cook to take home.

'Is it *svoboda* again?' I asked her on the way back.

'Ah Miss—what freedom is there in setting houses on fire? It is mad that they are—'

'Who?'

She merely shrugged.

But when spring gave way to summer, I found it was still possible to wander about, no policeman accosting me. Being so obviously a minor, I did not have to carry any identity documents, and once only did a tumultuous breath brush past me.

It happened soon after my birthday in 1907. I had a little money to spend and decided to go to the Summer Gardens. *Svoboda* had not reached the pleasances of St Petersburg, and it certainly did not dance its violent measure up and down the wide blue Neva. The steamer was crowded, but nobody talked about fires, bombs or poison, and it was good to stand at the prow and to watch the dark green splendour of the Summer Gardens draw nearer and nearer. A barge-café was moored alongside and, having left the steamer, I permitted myself the luxury of three small meat patties, a couple of apples and a bottle of lemonade. The fat girl in a blue smock smiled at me, and I smiled back. It would be such a perfect morning, I thought, crossing to the garden gates and making straight for the lilac arbour facing the Swan Stream. The swans came gliding up to the bank. They were too proud to beg, but they had one of the patties and an apple.

Then I settled down in the shade, opened my tattered copy of *The Wide Wide World* and was lost in it until hunger stirred in me. I enjoyed the food and then realized that, with my exchequer at zero, I would have to tramp home on foot. I crossed Mars Meadow by Suvorov's monument and reached Palace Quay, walking fast on the side nearest the river until I reached the Wladimir Palace. All the others had their windows shuttered, the owners being either abroad or gone to their country places. But the Wladimir Palace seemed very much alive. All its windows were unshuttered, and some were wide open. An elegant carriage drawn by two chestnuts stood by the front door. I halted and stared. From the first floor window appeared an arm in a lilac sleeve edged with lace, the July sun striking brilliant flashes from the emeralds and diamonds on wrist and fingers. I stared, fascinated by the splendour.

'Goodness! Is it the Grand-Duchess Wladimir? What is she doing in the city in the summer?'

I stood still and looked when suddenly a loud and gruff voice rang out behind. I turned to see a giant gendarme, his clean-shaven face anything but friendly.

'What are you doing here?' boomed the voice.

The man did not add '*Baryshna*' (Miss), and I could not blame him. My straw hat was shabby and its ribbon faded and frayed in several places; my pink gingham dress looked anything but fresh, and two hours' sprawl under the lilacs had not exactly improved it. My canvas shoes looked what they were—cheap, unshapely and well-worn. Altogether, the aristocratic Palace Quay and I could have nothing to say to each other. I halted, cheeks crimson, and pride alone prevented me from telling the gendarme that a cousin of my mother's was Mistress of the Robes to the Empress.

'Doing here?' I echoed rather woodenly. 'Why, I was only looking—'

In a flash the man produced his notebook.

'Name and address—' he commanded rather than asked.

I spelt the surname carefully and added the address. I could see that the former said nothing to the man. The latter made him curl his lip in contempt.

'And what were you looking at?' he wanted to know.

That seemed easy enough to answer.

'Why, the opened window, someone's arm in a lilac sleeve, and sunlight playing on the jewels—'

The gendarme broke in impatiently:

'You just go on, get to your home and don't forget that it is not healthy for anyone to loiter along Palace Quay. Understand?'

I heard, and pride gave way to anger.

'Well, I'll certainly tell my cousin all about it—'

'Your cousin—' he echoed, and I moved off saying over my shoulder:

'She happens to be one of the maids of honour to the Grand-Duchess Wladimir.'

He came out with a rude Russian equivalent of 'tell that to the Marines', but I ran off too fast for him to catch up with me.

That little incident left a sediment out of all proportion to its silliness and unimportance. Never again did I 'loiter' either up or down Palace Quay. In fact, for quite a time I avoided it altogether. The Summer Gardens could not be forsaken but there I would rather go by boat, when the exchequer allowed it, or else walk down the long Millionnaya Street at the back of Palace Quay.

Discontent expressing itself in terms of strikes, marches of University students and factory people, red flags waving above their heads, and very occasional provocative remarks overheard in some street or other, such was the visible pattern of tumult in my childhood and early teens. I was not encouraged to read the newspapers, and not till I was older would I learn about the heavy hand of censorship falling upon any piece of political news considered 'dangerous' by the authorities. I dimly sensed that *svoboda* meant freedom from misery, penury and hunger but, little by little, as I grew better acquainted with some of the slums, I came to understand that *svoboda* included much more than purely material relief: people wanted freedom to express themselves and to lead their lives unhampered by the intrusion of bureaucratic curiosity. I understood it, and yet it puzzled me: having known both poverty and hunger, I imagined them to be the bitterest enemies of mankind.

*

In the autumn of 1913 I entered the Xeniinsky where the least political discussion was strictly taboo and a heavy emphasis was laid on loyalty to the Imperial régime. That emphasis annoyed me because I thought it wholly unnecessary: like the rest of my family I took that loyalty for granted. We neither discussed it not questioned it. It seemed something as ordinary as brushing one's teeth in the morning.

But at the Xeniinsky 'loyalty' was something so heavily tinged with vapid sentimentality, so charged with a purely emotional idea about this and that member of the dynasty that I felt as though I were being kept in a monarchist hothouse, and an innocent remark of mine 'after all they are men and women like ourselves—except for their blood' led a *dame de classe* to suspect me of leftism! A discussion with my mother, however, allayed the suspicion, though I realized quickly enough that I had better keep to myself what impressions were left by visits to Maly Prospect and the Gavan.

The 1914 war started brilliantly for Russia, and each new victory would be celebrated by Te Deums, fireworks and illuminations. The scene witnessed from a window in Palace Square became more and more of a landmark in the mind. That, I then thought, was loyalty at its finest and best: loyalty to a great dynasty rather than to a person.

Yet those early victories were soon screened off by one crashing defeat after another. Te Deums gave way to requiems, and the mood at the front soon enough seeped into St Petersburg, with an incident at the Xeniinsky early in 1916 coming as a never-to-be-forgotten shock. I was then in the Upper First and had for some months enjoyed the friendship of a girl with an unusually fine mind and a passion for literature. One morning she was called out of the classroom and did not return. Just before luncheon, the form mistress said that my friend had been expelled for very grave reasons and that none of us were to mention her name. Naturally, the matter was discussed in every corner.

My friend's home was in the Crimea. The railways were by

then in a sad state, fewer and fewer 'civilian' trains running every week. I wrote to the Crimea, asking her to reply to my home address. There was no answer, and not until the Easter holidays did I meet her in a very dismal bakery in the 20th Line of Vassily Island. She was there as an assistant. Shortages being then the order of the day, there were about two dozen barley loaves for her to sell. I waited for the last customer to go before I burst out:

'Whatever made them expel you?'

She shrugged.

'They discovered that my father kept in touch with some people in Switzerland. He made no secret of it. He was wholly in sympathy with them.'

'With whom?'

'Here they call them revolutionaries—' she replied calmly.

I stared: before his retirement her father had held an important position at Court.

'Why didn't you go to the Crimea?'

'I had no money for the ticket. Besides, I have no home there —now—' she added. 'You see, the police arrested him one night. How could they keep me at the Xeniinsky after that? I was lucky to get this job.'

'Where is your father now?'

'He is dead—' she said tersely. 'I am sorry but I must close the shop.'

Smitten by dumbness, I went. She and I were never to meet again. But apparently whatever 'ideas' she had had were not found acceptable after October 1917. Her Christian name and surname, one of the most ancient untitled names in Russia, would appear in one of the very few lists issued at the time as 'liquidated', i.e. executed.

By the middle of 1916 a new detail entered the landscape of St Petersburg. It did not interfere with the beauty, but it did not add to it. It came to be known as *khvost* (literally, 'tail'), the queue. A *khvost* threaded its way along every street on Vassily Island. Often enough people would join it without having the least idea what it was they were queueing for. A newcomer might ask a question from the person in front and get a shrug for an answer. St Petersburg queued up for everything from clothing and lamp oil to a morsel of suspicious-looking meat and a pound of carrots. St Andrew's Market acquired a strange 'new look': people went there not so much to buy as to sell any junk they possessed from a small bookcase to a piece of lace. But there were few purchasers for such things, and every *khalat* had vanished.

The railway chaos grew and spread. In Michael Street just off the Nevsky stood a huge building, once a stockbroker's offices, now the Railway Ticket Bureau. Whatever the weather, the *kvost* there was sometimes five deep and stretched back to Nevsky Prospect. Those were the people both high-and-low born with enough money to buy their release from the catastrophe to come. Most of them went either north, to Finland, crossing the Norwegian frontier at Haparanda, or into the deep South, to the Crimea or the Caucasus.

Rationing came in too late and very patchily. But the black market flourished like a bay tree. Expensive restaurants were open and, as I heard, charged dizzy prices for the smallest meal. On the Nevsky, food shops stayed open to sell delicacies none but the wealthy could buy, but places like Alexandre's, Cabassue's and Knopf's were empty.

The *khvost* grew from a habit to a necessity, and stamped itself upon the people. Newspapers still came out but comparatively few bought them: the *khvost* became their paper, club, library—all in one. People did all they could to shorten the hours of waiting by chatter, and most fantastic rumours spread like weeds in a neglected garden. Police still patrolled the South Bank waterfront, the Nevsky and most of the adjoining streets, but they did not trouble themselves about the *khvosty* in the humbler parts of the city.

The rumours swelled; standing in one of those queues one morning in early January of 1917 I heard that the war with Germany was finished and that it was raging bitterly, that China had attacked Siberia, that the Imperial family had left Tsarskoe Selo for England, that the Allies had betrayed us, and so on. Then the chatter would plunge into domestic, more immediate waters. Three trains, loaded with grain and fats for St Petersburg, had been delivered nobody knew where and the entire freight sold—to the Austrians. An ugly word crept more and more often into the *khvost* chatter: *izmena* (treason), and 'traitors' were named within the strangely frightening liberty of speech: from the Empress Alexandra down to an otherwise insignificant corn merchant, cruelly mishandled by an angry hungry crowd somewhere on Petersburg Side. The ugly little word became a relief, a challenge, and a forerunner of the trouble to come.

The city kept her matchless beauty; the brief wintry days would close in a soft rose-golden glory none but a genius could have caught on the canvas. The waters of the Neva were deep in slumber. The snow lay undisturbed: there was neither time nor labour to deal with the drifts. Unaccustomed hands of men, women and even children dealt with them after a particularly sharp blizzard. The municipality acknowledged their labour and paid those people at pre-war rates. Three hours' work enabled you to buy a couple of frozen herrings or a pound of potatoes, and you considered yourself lucky.

Warmth and food became the two major needs. Stacks of logs needed for the stoves grew smaller and smaller, and occasionally would be replenished by most illegal and revolting methods. To hack rowing boats to pieces was bad enough, but to slink at dead of night to the nearest cemetery and to fill whole sacks with the wooden crosses from the graves of poor folk suggested something out of all accord with earlier accepted decency.

Then, little by little, rioting started. The first riot broke out at the door of a humble little bakery on Maly Prospect. The *khvost* about to form became aware of the shuttered windows and the barred door. Within an instant the door and the windows were splintered to pieces. The *khvost* soon became a mob. The mounted police did not hurry but we heard they arrived in time to save the lives of the old baker and his wife. The couple were taken into comparative safety; the mob dispersed and became a *khvost* somewhere else. But that morning remained a landmark in the memory of many people.

*

There came a day in late February (O.S.) 1917 when my mother's wealthiest pupil arrived with her husband, their arms laden with most heterogenous parcels; they were leaving for Odessa later in the evening and brought us what looked like the entire contents of their larder, not forgetting to add two tin-openers. They were in a hurry to go, and our gratitude must have seemed rather inadequate, so bewildered were we by such boundless generosity. Left alone, we arranged all the treasures as tidily as we could in the small space at our disposal, their parting words still ringing in our ears:

'Keep indoors for a few days. Something is about to happen —and that very soon. Most of the gendarmes and the police have gone into hiding.'

Something happened before the day had died. That night my mother and I never went to bed. We sat by the window and watched one enormous shower of flames after another rise to the wintry skies over the South Bank. We did not know the details at the time, but many private houses were being set on fire. *Litowsky Zamok,* the grim old prison on the bank of the Moyka, was burning, all the prisoners having been let out. So was St Nicholas' Hospital, its bewildered inmates pushed into a freedom their clouded minds could neither use nor understand.

Shortly after midnight, our floormaid, a big bundle in her hands, appeared in the doorway.

'I am going to my village near Moscow,' she said crisply. 'There are twelve of us in this house alone! No more scrubbing!' she giggled. 'We are all equal now! *Svboda* has come this time and no mistake—'

'But how are you going to manage?'

'Ah, there are still a few trains from Nicholas Station. We mean to fight our way through, no policeman pushing us back.'

'It is a very long way to walk from here,' remarked my mother, and the girl giggled again.

'Walk? Why should we walk? Plenty of lorries about to give a lift to honest peasant women.'

She went without saying goodbye. She had been a good worker, though slightly light-fingered, but we were not sorry to see her go.

After a few minutes we crept out into the wide passage, its windows facing Bolshoy Boulevard. The night should have been Stygian dark. Now you could have read small print in the passage. Right opposite, the police station was in flames from end to end. A little to the left, a big private house, with a garden in front and in the rear had been set on fire. The trees in front had already been burnt down to their stumps, and the house was a huge bonfire from its ground floor to the rear. Down below hurrying figures were now caught in that illumination, now vanished in the shadows. Red on black, black on gold and red. . . . It all suggested a décor to a Wagnerian opera. Lorries, carrying armed men, clattered past on the icy cobbles. There came a violent crash, and the big private house shuddered and collapsed, wholly surrendered to the onslaught of fire and smoke. In silence, we turned back to our room and the window facing the South Bank. There were many more fires. The room was flooded by the angry light.

The revolution was leaping through its initial stage and Russia was no longer an Empire. A temporary government was being formed at Taurida Palace, but through that night and for many days to come the mob did not concern itself with any government. St Petersburg was under its will, which expressed itself in looting, murder and arson.

Svoboda, a startling red-hooded figure was there, and its birthpangs brought no mercy to the very same people it had meant to rescue from all tyranny and misery, i.e. the poor of St Petersburg, who were to suffer most from hunger, cold and a choking sense of helplessness. Later, the high temper quietened down, and *svoboda* was indeed enjoyed for a few brief months until the October days of 1917 strangled its breath.

But a differently coloured tyranny could not break St Petersburg. Much of its man-made beauty had indeed perished, but much more remained, and no upheaval, however destructive, could interfere with the city's identity. That St Petersburg kept inviolate. As strong as the granite girdle along the Neva banks, it stood, poised far above all untoward circumstance, its beauty and strength comforting and sustaining many.

CHAPTER FOURTEEN

Epilogue

I HAVE tried to tell the story of St Petersburg as I learnt and experienced it during my early years. I know I shall never again see the city, but neither time nor distance should have the power to dwarf the allegiance and love grown since childhood. A place once truly loved stands high above all the inevitable changes brought about by the greedy corrosion of Time, the destructive wrath of a mob, and, finally, the sad evidences of war ravages.

St Petersburg was created by a genius who had small use for arts, but the city, evoked out of the swamp, could never become utilitarian for all her docks, mills and factories. She was a poem of stone, water and wind, and no Russian-born painter had ever done her justice. Giorgione and Leonardo would have been able to interpret her pale green, pearl-grey and lilac distances. Of all the Russian poets, Pushkin alone sang her beauty, but Pushkin had wildly alien blood on his mother's side. Of all the great Russian composers, Tchaikovsky alone was enabled to catch some of her moods, but the great Germans,

exander Pushkin

Wagner in particular, would have found a home in her heart.

So, in the end, Peter the Great's purpose in 'opening a window to the West' came to be fulfilled in the language of artists. His creation was at once delicate and brutal, and so, it stayed in the years when I lived there: incredible splendour brushing against appalling squalor, great riches neighboured by stark penury. But the pulse of the city beat steadily through all the divergences, and her climate evoked so much, her skies frowned and smiled, her waters invited and repelled, and each of the four seasons offered enough to shape the qualities of heart and mind.

Sometimes her accents were as soft as the mossy slopes of her many pleasances. Again, they would be as hard as the blocks of Finnish granite gone to the making of parapets for the Neva, its temper so uncertain, its beauty leaving you beggared of words.

St Petersburg was an incredible contradiction. Her trade flourished for all the Gulf of Finland stayed ice-shackled for five months of the year, but she was never 'mercantile' in the sense of Lübeck, Hamburg or Hull. She was the capital of a proud Empire and she also belonged to the world, and had a smile for any foreigner come to make his fortune on the islands. She had admittedly Russian streaks—such as the famous Palkin's on Nevsky Prospect where you were served with creamed 'bortch' and Pozharsky cutlets, and would imagine yourself in Moscow until a pink-cheeked maître d'hôtel brought you the bill and thanked you for your patronage in accents which made you think of Riga or Königsberg, never of Moscow.

First and foremost, the city was herself; all the hardihoods, secrets, tragedies and raptures she offered, came out of her own mint. And, somehow, across the trek of many years, the raptures stand in the foreground: the delight of the first snow-fall, the lilacs breaking into bud, the regal course of the great river, and the scent of lime blossoms in the Summer Gardens—together with innumerable kindnesses of men and women up and down the social ladder.

These remain; and within them all is the city, at once a secret and a revelation, a tender mother and a stern mistress. To remember even a corner of that landscape has been a joy and a refreshment.